Project Management Institute

Government Extension to the PMBOK® Guide
Third Edition

Government Extension to the PMBOK® Guide Third Edition

ISBN 13: 978-1-930699-91-5
ISBN 10: 1-930699-91-3

Published by: Project Management Institute, Inc.
Four Campus Boulevard
Newtown Square, Pennsylvania 19073-3299 USA.
Phone: +610-356-4600
Fax: +610-356-4647
E-mail: pmihq@pmi.org
Internet: www.pmi.org

Notice

The Project Management Institute, Inc. (PMI) standards and guideline publications, of which the document contained herein is one, are developed through a voluntary consensus standards development process. This process brings together volunteers and/or seeks out the views of persons who have an interest in the topic covered by this publication. While PMI administers the process and establishes rules to promote fairness in the development of consensus, it does not write the document and it does not independently test, evaluate, or verify the accuracy or completeness of any information or the soundness of any judgments contained in its standards and guideline publications.

PMI disclaims liability for any personal injury, property or other damages of any nature whatsoever, whether special, indirect, consequential or compensatory, directly or indirectly resulting from the publication, use of application, or reliance on this document. PMI disclaims and makes no guaranty or warranty, expressed or implied, as to the accuracy or completeness of any information published herein, and disclaims and makes no warranty that the information in this document will fulfill any of your particular purposes or needs. PMI does not undertake to guarantee the performance of any individual manufacturer or seller's products or services by virtue of this standard or guide.

In publishing and making this document available, PMI is not undertaking to render professional or other services for or on behalf of any person or entity, nor is PMI undertaking to perform any duty owed by any person or entity to someone else. Anyone using this document should rely on his or her own independent judgment or, as appropriate, seek the advice of a competent professional in determining the exercise of reasonable care in any given circumstances. Information and other standards on the topic covered by this publication may be available from other sources, which the user may wish to consult for additional views or information not covered by this publication.

PMI has no power, nor does it undertake to police or enforce compliance with the contents of this document. PMI does not certify, tests, or inspect products, designs, or installations for safety or health purposes. Any certification or other statement of compliance with any health or safety-related information in this document shall not be attributable to PMI and is solely the responsibility of the certifier or maker of the statement.

Contents

List of Figures

Preface

The *Government Extension to the PMBOK® Guide Third Edition* is the first industry-specific extension to *A Guide to the Project Management Body of Knowledge (PMBOK® Guide)*. It provides information on managing projects within the unique environment of the public sector. The term "public sector" refers to national, regional and local governments. This update expands the scope of the previous edition to include all forms of government. It supersedes the *Government Extension to A PMBOK® Guide—2000 Edition* and is aligned with, and a supplement to, the *PMBOK® Guide—Third Edition* and should be used in conjunction with it. The alignment enables easier reference to the corresponding sections in each document. The process names and designations were updated to match the changes introduced in the current edition of *PMBOK® Guide* in order to enable consistency and clarity.

The *PMBOK® Guide* describes knowledge and practices "generally recognized as good practices" and applicable to "most of the projects, most of the time" and for which there is wide spread consensus about their value and usefulness. As an extension, this document builds upon the *PMBOK® Guide—Third Edition* by describing additional knowledge and practices, and by modifying some of them.

Some changes were made in this edition to update and align this global standard to the *PMBOK® Guide—Third Edition*. A discussion of changes made in this edition can be found in Appendix A.

Section I

The Project Management Framework

Chapter 1

Introduction

PMI's *A Guide to the Project Management Body of Knowledge*—Third Edition describes the Project Management Body of Knowledge as "the sum of knowledge within the profession of project management" that resides with practitioners and academics who apply and advance it. While the *PMBOK® Guide*—Third Edition provides a generic foundation for managing projects in the public and private sectors, this document addresses the specific practices found in public sector projects. This document supersedes the previous edition of the Government Extension, entitled *Government Extension to the PMBOK® Guide—2000 Edition.*

This extension to the *PMBOK® Guide*—Third Edition provides an overview of key attributes of project governance that apply to most public sector organizations and that are "generally recognized as good practice . . . applicable to most projects most of the time," and with "widespread consensus about their value and usefulness." It establishes a framework for ensuring effective and efficient management of projects in the public sector. It does not, however, provide practices or guidance that should be uniformly applied on all projects. The project management team is ultimately responsible for determining what is appropriate for any given project.

Readers should note that, while many of the references used in the *Government Extension* are derived from the *PMBOK® Guide*—Third Edition, its content is specifically designed to suit the unique characteristics of projects in the government sector. Project management professionals should plan to use both documents concurrently in the execution of their responsibilities. To that end, this chapter is organized into the following sections to reflect the structure of the *PMBOK® Guide*—Third Edition:

1.1 **Purpose of the *Government Extension***
1.2 **What is a Project?**
1.3 **Project Management in the Government Context**
1.4 **Structure of the *Government Extension***
1.5 **Areas of Expertise**
1.6 **Project Management Context**
1.7 **Explanation of *Government Extension* Processes: Inputs, Tools & Techniques, and Outputs**

1.1 Purpose of the *Government Extension*

The *PMBOK® Guide*—Third Edition sets forth the subset of the Project Management Body of Knowledge that is generally recognized as good practice. It provides an overview of practices that apply to most projects most of the time, and for which there is widespread consensus about their value and usefulness. The concept of good practice implies that the correct application of skills, tools, and techniques not only can increase the chances of project success, but can be extended to many diverse application areas.

The *Government Extension* interprets and extends the precepts of proficient project management found in the *PMBOK® Guide*—Third Edition to public sector entities. The key characteristics of public sector projects are listed in Section 1.3 of this chapter.

Appendix D of the *PMBOK® Guide*—Third Edition describes application area extensions. Application area extensions are necessary when there are generally accepted knowledge and practices for a category of projects in one application area that are not generally accepted across the full range of project types in most application areas. Application areas reflect:

- Unique or unusual aspects of the project environment of which the project management team must be aware in order to manage the project efficiently and effectively
- Common knowledge and practices that, if followed, will improve the efficiency and effectiveness of a project (e.g., standard work breakdown structures).

Projects undertaken by government organizations are primarily funded by and executed for the benefit of citizens, rather than for financial results. To this extent, the focus of the *Government Extension to the PMBOK® Guide*—Third Edition centers on two distinguishing factors peculiar to public sector organizations that can affect project governance:

- The law which stipulates precise terms for the execution and enforcement of fiduciary, managerial, and sociopolitical responsibilities
- Responsibility of the project team to serve as stewards of the public interest

This Government Extension provides a framework for improving the management of public sector projects. The recommendations presented here are focused on providing guidance in managing the intricacies of government project specifics. They provide guiding principles for ensuring the efficiency and effectiveness of project controls to allow accountability to a nation's citizens, as required by public law.

1.1.1 Audience for the Government Extension to the PMBOK® Guide Third Edition

This extension serves as a foundational reference for anyone involved in or with the profession of project management, working for or doing business with public sector organizations. This includes, but is not limited to:

- Political leaders
- Senior executives
- Program managers and managers of project managers
- Project managers and other project team members
- Members of a project management office
- Customers and other stakeholders
- Functional managers with employees assigned to project teams
- Internal and external auditors, and project personnel who define and assess project controls
- Educators teaching project management and other related subjects
- Consultants and other specialists in the project management and related fields

- Trainers developing project management educational programs
- Researchers analyzing project management.

1.2 What Is a Project?

See Section 1.2 of the *PMBOK® Guide*—Third Edition.

1.2.1 Project Characteristics

See Section 1.2.1 of the *PMBOK® Guide*—Third Edition.

1.2.2 Projects vs. Operational Work

See Section 1.2.2 of the *PMBOK® Guide*—Third Edition.

1.2.3 Projects and Strategic Planning

See Section 1.2.3 of the *PMBOK® Guide*—Third Edition.

1.2.4 Why are Government Projects Unique?

Government projects are generally considered to have unique characteristics from those in the private sector. The project management team must recognize the following unique characteristics in order to manage the project efficiently and effectively:

- Legal constraints on government projects
- Accountability to the public
- Utilization of public resources

.1 **Legal Constraints on Government Projects**

Although private sector projects may be subject to certain laws and regulations, government projects are generally subject to additional laws and regulations that can significantly impact government projects. Government bodies establish laws and regulations that set clear limits on the government body, the executive leadership, and the ministries, agencies, and departments. To proceed beyond these limits, government officials generally must obtain permission from the government body or from an administrative body having delegated authority. If granted, this permission can take the form of a change in the law or a waiver of a legal requirement.

.2 **Accountability to the Public**

In private sector projects, project managers are accountable to the immediate client and a limited number of stakeholders such as shareholders, employees, etc. However, in government projects, the project managers are accountable to many stakeholders beyond the immediate client. In the public sector, participants in the accountability process are internal and external to the government body. Internal participants can include various members of the government body including the executive leadership and representatives of ministries, agencies, and departments, as well as employees. External participants include members of the public, special interest groups, the press, and other levels of government. All of these participants in the accountability process may have the right to challenge or protest decisions made by project managers in public sector projects.

.3 Utilization of Public Resources

Government budgets are funded with public resources that come from *mandatory* taxes, bonds, and other fees that require budget authority to obligate and subsequently spend, or outlay, the funds. Execution of budget authority is generally a three-step process:

- Funds are *committed* through a budget resolution that reflects consensus of the legislative body
- Funds are *obligated* when a procurement action is undertaken
- Funds are *outlaid* when the goods are delivered or services are rendered.

The project manager has a duty to use the public funds to meet the goals set by government bodies. The approval and budgeting process, as well as financial and scope control mechanisms, help to ensure that the expenditure of funds collected from mandatory taxes, bonds, and fees complies with applicable laws and regulations, and that funds are well utilized to provide better public service for the citizens. Although Benefits Cost Analysis (BCA) and Return on Investment (ROI) are sometimes used in the public sector to evaluate government projects, project success is more often measured in benefits to the public rather than revenue or cost savings to the government body.

Project decisions should be guided by professional judgment consistent with the public interest and trust. Officials, project managers, and auditors are entrusted with the responsibility to ensure that public resources are used efficiently and effectively.

1.3 Project Management in the Government Context

The *PMBOK® Guide*—Third Edition characterizes program management as "the centralized, coordinated management of a group of projects to achieve the program's strategic objectives and benefits." Their strong focus on strategic planning distinguishes such projects from more tactical projects.

In the private sector, projects are aligned with strategic plans and company objectives, and may be part of programs or portfolios. In large companies, such project hierarchies are formalized most of the time, whereas in small or mid-size organizations, the projects might only have implicit interdependencies.

1.3.1 Levels of Government

This extension applies to three generally recognized levels of government. What follows are representative descriptions of those levels that are widely recognized around the globe. It is not meant to be an exhaustive description of all levels of government worldwide.

- **National government.** The government of an internationally recognized country. Generally the country will be a confederation or a federation of regional governments defined below, or a unitary state.
- **Regional government.** The government of a portion of a large country with a national government. In small countries, there may not be any regional governments—only a national government and local governments. Regional governments are called by many different terms, including but not limited to: states, provinces, landers, departments, cantons, principalities, republics, territories, etc.

- **Local government.** The government of a small portion of a country or region. There are sometimes overlapping local governments with different duties. Local governments are called by many different terms, including but not limited to: counties, cities, towns, municipalities, prefectures, boroughs, shires, etc.

1.3.2 Project and Stakeholder Interdependencies

Government projects are determined by the government's agenda, and have to be approved and budgeted in advance. Government project are not normally analyzed on an individual basis; for larger bodies (such as national and regional governments), it is more practical to group them as programs from a budgeting and control perspective. The long approval and budgeting cycles require government projects to be much more strategically oriented than private sector ones.

In the public sector, not only is there a higher percentage of projects that are part of programs than in the private sector, but project interdependencies are more clearly identified and documented. The governance and management flows hierarchically from political agenda items down to the execution level (as represented by projects).

In most cases, the stakeholders involved at each level represent and draw authority from the stakeholders involved at the upper level in the hierarchy. For example, if a government agenda item requires cooperation at the program level from two agencies, the specific branches or divisions and stakeholders within each agency would be involved.

Indeed, the lower hierarchical levels will have additional stakeholders with no representation at the upper levels, such as interest-specific citizens' groups or third parties involved in project execution. Nonetheless, almost every project has a core group of stakeholders with representation at higher levels. This provides project stability and alignment to program and higher levels, but could also create dramatic impacts generated by external factors, such as government or political direction changes.

1.4 Structure of the *Government Extension*

The *Government Extension to the PMBOK® Guide Third Edition* is organized into the following three sections:
- The Project Management Framework
- The Standard for Project Management of a Project
- The Project Management Knowledge Areas.

1.4.1 Section I:—The Project Management Framework

Section 1, "The Project Management Framework," provides a basic structure for understanding project management in the government sector.

Chapter 1, **Introduction**, defines key terms and provides an overview for the rest of the *Government Extension*.

Chapter 2, **Project Life Cycle and Organization**, describes the environment in which government projects operate. The project management team should understand this broader context. Managing the day-to-day activities of the project is necessary, but not sufficient, to ensure success.

1.4.2 Section II:—The Standard for Project Management of a Project

Section II, "The Standard for Project Management of a Project," specifies all the project management processes that are used by the project team to manage a government project.

Chapter 3, **Project Management Processes for a Project**, describes the five required Project Management Process Groups for any project and their constituent project management processes. This chapter describes the multidimensional nature of project management.

1.4.3 Section III:—The Project Management Knowledge Areas

Section III, "The Project Management Knowledge Areas," organizes the forty-four project management processes from Chapter 3's Project Management Process Groups into nine Knowledge Areas. An introduction to Section III describes the legend for the process flow diagrams used in each Knowledge Area chapter, and also provides introductory material applicable to all nine Knowledge Areas.

Chapter 4, **Project Integration Management**, describes the processes and activities that integrate the various elements of project management that are identified, defined, combined, unified, and coordinated within the Project Management Process Groups. It consists of the Develop Project Charter, Develop Preliminary Project Scope Statement, Develop Project Management Plan, Direct and Manage Project Execution, Monitor and Control Project Work, Integrated Change Control, and Close Project project management processes.

Chapter 5, **Project Scope Management**, describes the processes involved in ascertaining that the project includes all the work required, and only the work required, to complete the project successfully. It consists of the Scope Planning, Scope Definition, Create Work Breakdown Structure (WBS), Scope Verification, and Scope Control project management processes.

Chapter 6, **Project Time Management**, describes the processes concerning the timely completion of the project. It consists of the Activity Definition, Activity Sequencing, Activity Resource Estimating, Activity Duration Estimating, Schedule Development, and Schedule Control project management processes.

Chapter 7, **Project Cost Management**, describes the processes involved in planning, estimating, budgeting, and controlling costs so that the project is completed within the approved budget. It consists of the Cost Estimating, Cost Budgeting, and Cost Control project management processes.

Chapter 8, **Project Quality Management**, describes the processes involved in assuring that the project will satisfy the objectives for which it was undertaken. It consists of the Quality Planning, Perform Quality Assurance, and Perform Quality Control project management processes.

Chapter 9, **Project Human Resource Management**, describes the processes that organize and manage the project team. It consists of the Human Resource Planning, Acquire Project Team, Develop Project Team, and Manage Project Team project management processes.

Chapter 10, **Project Communications Management**, describes the processes concerning the timely and appropriate generation, collection, dissemination, storage, and ultimate disposition of project information. It consists of the Communications Planning, Information Distribution, Performance Reporting, and Manage Stakeholders project management processes.

Chapter 11, **Project Risk Management**, describes the processes concerned with conducting risk management on a project. It consists of the Risk Management Planning, Risk Identification, Qualitative Risk Analysis, Quantitative Risk Analysis, Risk Response Planning, and Risk Monitoring and Control project management processes.

Chapter 12, **Project Procurement Management**, describes the processes that purchase or acquire products, services or results, as well as contract management processes. It consists of the Plan Purchases and Acquisitions, Plan Contracting, Request Seller Responses, Select Sellers, Contract Administration, and Contract Closure project management processes.

1.5 Areas of Expertise

See Section 1.5 of the *PMBOK® Guide*—Third Edition.

1.5.1 Project Management Body of Knowledge

See Section 1.5.1 of the *PMBOK® Guide*—Third Edition.

1.5.2 Application Area Knowledge, Standards, and Regulations

See Section 1.5.2 of the *PMBOK® Guide*—Third Edition.

1.5.3 Understanding the Project Environment

See Section 1.5.3 of the *PMBOK® Guide*—Third Edition.

1.5.4 General Management Knowledge and Skills

See Section 1.5.4 of the *PMBOK® Guide*—Third Edition.

1.5.5 Interpersonal Skills

See Section 1.5.5 of the *PMBOK® Guide*—Third Edition.

1.6 Project Management Context

See Section 1.6 of the *PMBOK® Guide*—Third Edition.

1.6.1 Programs and Program Management

See Section 1.6.1 of the *PMBOK® Guide*—Third Edition, with an understanding that programs are generally more common in government than in the private sector. In government programs, there is often far more emphasis on the ongoing operations described in the *PMBOK® Guide*—Third Edition definition and, in some cases, some government bodies classify ongoing operations themselves as a program. Further, some governments also treat programs like portfolios of projects. Unlike commercial programs, government programs are used to set social goals, provide social services, and set priorities through public discourse (meetings and voting) and accountability (audits, hearings, legal actions, and the press).

Government bodies, especially larger governments, generally appropriate funds to programs rather than to individual projects. On regional or national levels, the legislative body sets program goals and priorities but can not review the details of every project. For example, such bodies may appropriate funds for a program of school improvements, with rules for how the funds are to be divided among individual projects. The government body has the authority to fund and then later redirect (reprogram) program funding to other purposes, provided there is a majority in agreement to do so.

On the other hand, in smaller governments, the legislative body may appropriate funds for individual projects and/or programs. A local body may, for instance, appropriate funds for an individual project involving a new classroom at a local school or a program for school improvements. The use of public funding, public accountability and setting of social goals that are measured in social good rather than return on investment make government programs unique.

1.6.2 Portfolios and Portfolio Management

See Section 1.6.2 of the *PMBOK® Guide*—Third Edition, with an understanding that portfolios of projects are very common in smaller government bodies where each project can be approved, funded, and monitored individually. Managing and monitoring them as portfolios allows the budgetary authority to have an overall view of the entire budget execution, and redistribute funds as needed to achieve maximum benefits for their constituents.

1.6.3 Subprojects

See Section 1.6.3 of the *PMBOK® Guide*—Third Edition.

1.6.4 Project Management Office

See Section 1.6.4 of the *PMBOK® Guide*—Third Edition.

1.7 Explanation of *Government Extension* Processes: Inputs, Tools & Techniques, and Outputs

This document follows closely the structure and organization of the *PMBOK® Guide*—Third Edition. This enables easier cross-referencing between equivalent sections of this extension and the *PMBOK® Guide*.

The *PMBOK® Guide*—Third Edition describes the inputs, tools and techniques, and outputs of each project management process. For each process, it includes a table that lists three types of elements. This document includes similar tables. In each table, the elements have the following format:

- Elements that remain unchanged from the *PMBOK® Guide*—Third Edition are shown in plain text.
- New items are shown in ***bold italics***
- Changed elements are shown in *italics*.

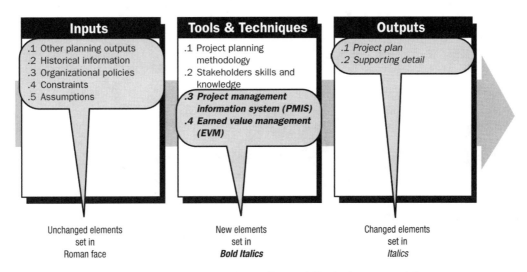

Figure 1-1. Identification of Revised Inputs, Tools & Techniques, and Outputs

Chapter 2

Project Life Cycle and Organization

The *PMBOK® Guide*—Third Edition advises that "Projects and project management are carried out in an environment broader than that of the project itself." Chapter 2 of the *Government Extension* describes some of the unique features of this environment for government projects.

2.1 The Project Life Cycle

A responsible government body will require an executive to submit intermediate deliverables during project development. The phases of government projects often correspond to these deliverables. Government construction projects, for instance, typically have the three phases with subphases as shown in Figure 2-1. Each phase in this example is required by a law adopted by the legislative body.

Origination

　　1. Origination document, used to obtain funding.

Planning and Design

　　1. Alternative selection (planning), which is often controlled by environmental law. For example, on United States government projects, alternative selection is controlled by the National Environmental Policy Act.

　　2. Bid documents (design), controlled by public law.

Procurement

　　1. Property acquisition, using eminent domain law.

　　2. Construction, controlled by public contract law.

Figure 2-1. Typical Phases of a Government Construction Project

2.1.1 Characteristics of the Project Life Cycle

See Section 2.1.1 of the *PMBOK® Guide*—Third Edition.

2.1.2 Characteristics of Project Phases

See Section 2.1.2 of the *PMBOK® Guide*—Third Edition for an explanation of project phases.

One phase that is especially common in public sector projects is the origination phase, described below:

.1 Origination Phase

Every government project begins with an origination phase. The written product of this phase is called by many different names. These names include feasibility study report, basic planning report, project study report, project concept report, project location report, budget proposal, and funding request.

The report, proposal, or funding request describes the product in sufficient detail to determine if the project should proceed. If there is a program of projects, the origination document is used to determine whether the project should be included in the program. (For a discussion of programs and program management, see Section 1.6.1.) If there is no program of projects, the government body must approve each project separately. In this case, the origination document is submitted by the executive to request funding.

The budget must include some discretionary funds for the executive to produce project proposals. Without this funding, the executive cannot legally propose new projects.

2.1.3 Project Life Cycle and Product Life Cycle Relationships

See Section 2.1.3 of the *PMBOK® Guide*—Third Edition.

2.2 Project Stakeholders

The *PMBOK® Guide*—Third Edition lists key stakeholders on every project, including the project manager, customer, performing organization, project team members, and sponsor. On government projects, the project manager, customer, and project team members are the same as on private sector projects. The performing organization is a department or agency that reports to the executive. The sponsor is either an executive official or a government body.

Government projects have several other key stakeholders:

- The general public. In addition to participation through their representative bodies, individuals and organizations may participate directly in a project through public hearings and reviews, as well as in lobbying efforts for and against the project, and for and against the various project alternatives.
- *Regulators.* These are individuals or organizations that must approve various aspects of the project. Regulators enforce rules and regulations. They are actively involved in the project, but generally have no interest in its success, since it will not affect them. Regulators are either agents of a higher government, or of another agency in the same government as the performing organization. Inadequate communication between the project manager and regulators can delay or even destroy a project.
  - National government projects are regulated by national government agencies. They are generally not subject to regulation by regional and local governments. National projects may also be regulated by international compacts such as the European Union, North American Free Trade Agreement (NAFTA), General Agree-

ment on Tariffs and Trade (GATT), and Convention on International Trade in Endangered Species (CITES).

- Regional government projects are subject to the same regulation as national government projects and are also regulated by other regional government agencies but are generally not subject to regulation by local governments.
- Local government projects are subject to the same regulation as regional government projects and are also regulated by other local government agencies.

- *Opposition Stakeholders.* Though not found in every project, this is a special class of stakeholders who perceive themselves as being harmed if the project is successful. An example is the homeowner who lives beside a park that is to be converted into a highway. Early involvement of opposition stakeholders may result in a more positive outcome for all stakeholders.
- *The Press.* In countries that have freely elected governments, the press is always present on major projects where large sums of money are involved. The press has a duty to report on the project in an objective manner, but often focuses more on problems than successes.
- *Sellers.* In the procurement process, these are often significant stakeholders. They are discussed in Chapter 12.
- *Future Generations.* During their limited tenure, governments have a responsibility to future generations regarding long-term debt, viable and affordable infrastructure, and a feasible environment.
- *The Private Sector.* The private sector provides counterpart funding and participates in public-private partnerships.

2.3 Organizational Influences

The organizational influences directly affecting government projects are determined by the type of government and how the officials are chosen. In elected governments, the voters elect representatives who establish laws, statutes, ordinances, regulations, and policies. The process is based upon consensus building with checks and balances in place to protect the stakeholders from fraud or abuse of power by the elected officials. The organizational system creates the environment for monitored, deliberate progress on a project. In this environment, clear limits are established, including roles and responsibilities for the project team, deliverables, funding resources and authority, the process for selecting and procuring necessary resources, and the necessary audit trail to successfully complete the project within schedule and budget.

The electoral cycle exerts an intense organizational influence on government projects and, consequently, projects must demonstrate policy success. If there is a change in the leadership of the government, there is the possibility of a reversal or change in policy, which can dramatically affect the life of the project. Also, the principle of civil service neutrality sometimes leads to decisions not being made if they could be interpreted as favoring one group versus another.

Another type of organizational influence for government projects exists in the area of historical information. Project decisions influenced by historical information must be carefully weighed against possible future changes in government leadership, policy, or methodology, since such changes can render historical information and decisions based on it as irrelevant.

2.3.1 Organizational Systems

The budgeting system and process for government projects are controlled by policy and law. Funds are budgeted for a specific time period. Projects compete for new funding for each fiscal year. Organizational systems and governance programs which ensure that projects meet the required standards for the government entity can cause delays in project progress and, in some cases, termination of the project due to expired funding.

Governance systems, including the use of Governance Boards, Change Control Boards, Configuration Management Boards, etc., are mandated by government entities to ensure proper use of taxpayer dollars and best value investment strategies.

Many times, the program office is separate from the project office. There must be an open and active communications system to keep any stakeholders informed of any potential changes to the status of the project and its ability to meet the requirements in fulfilling the mission of the organization.

The system of public scrutiny, allowing the public to hear both sides of the story, is necessary to ensure that the voter population is informed and understands both the advantages and disadvantages of the project.

The systems in place for government procurement are heavily regulated, and consequences for non-compliance can be severe, depending upon the nature of the violation.

The system for resolving conflicts, open issues, and change orders varies by organization, but is typically covered in the policies and guidelines published by the organization. If there is no existing remedy, there may be a requirement for new legislation or policy.

Systems for collecting, managing, and maintaining government records are required to meet the standards defined by law. The project archive must be maintained for the required number of years and in the required format as prescribed by governing records management standards.

2.3.2 Organizational Cultures and Styles

Communications requirements unique to government planning relate primarily to establishing a culture of information sharing in a functional bureaucracy. Government departments tend to be compartmentalized—not projectized. Therefore, when multi-agency communication will be required, consideration as to how this will be accomplished should be planned into the project.

In many organizations, performance contracts for project managers and team members are common. The contracts are linked to the relevant key performance indicators of the specific program being managed, and are monitored as part of the project evaluation reports. Performance measurement in government is likely to involve scrutiny by independent agencies (for example, the United States General Accountability Office).

The ability of citizens in many countries to view almost all government records, with a few non-absolute exceptions (prompted by secrecy and invasion of privacy laws), may restrict project managers in maintaining confidential information.

2.3.3 Organizational Structure

Organizational policies determine the functional-to-projectized structure used in managing government projects. The organization may only have specific powers (e.g., executive or legislative) assigned to it by the governmental leadership.

Also, different levels of government may have different and separate requirements for project approval. All of the requirements must be met by the project in order to gain approval.

A key feature of governments is the presence of opposition. Project managers should be aware that the project or the policy that causes the project to exist is likely to be subject to actively hostile scrutiny from the opposition.

Government policies will change during the course of a change in leadership. The merit-based civil service system is gaining popularity as a way to preserve neutrality in government service. Civil servants hold office from one administration to another, but they must remain politically neutral. For more discussion on the role of civil servants, see Chapter 9.

2.3.4 The Role of the PMO in Organizational Structures

Project management offices (PMOs) can be vital to the success of government projects. The ability to provide up-to-date source-driven project information can be very important to the continued life of the project and the successful transition from one project phase to another. Many government projects have multiple vendors, stakeholders, inspectors, etc. involved in the operations and oversight of the project activities, and these complex relationships would be more difficult to coordinate without a PMO. The use of a fully functioning PMO depends on the size and complexity of the project at hand.

A well-designed and developed PMO facilitates the active participation and review of all parties. It can also serve as the repository for all project records, including correspondence, memos, reports (written or electronic), presentations of content, and any other documents describing and detailing the project. This information may become available to the public.

2.3.5 Project Management System

See Section 2.3.5 in the *PMBOK® Guide*—Third Edition.

Section II

The Standard for Project Management of a Project

Chapter 3   Project Management Processes for a Project

Chapter 3

Project Management Processes for a Project

Project management in the government sector utilizes the same Project Management Process Groups as in the private sector. However, it should be noted that enterprise environmental factors in government require rigid application of certain processes to comply with laws and regulations.

See Chapter 3 in the *PMBOK® Guide*—Third Edition.

Section III

The Project Management Knowledge Areas

Chapter 4

Project Integration Management

According to the *PMBOK® Guide*—Third Edition, Project Integration Management includes "the processes and activities needed to identify, define, combine, unify, and coordinate the various processes and project management activities within the Project Management Process Groups." Chapter 4 of the *PMBOK® Guide*—Third Edition describes seven major integrative project management processes:

    4.1 Develop Project Charter
    4.2 Develop Preliminary Project Scope Statement
    4.3 Develop Project Management Plan
    4.4 Direct and Manage Project Execution
    4.5 Monitor and Control Project Work
    4.6 Integrated Change Control
    4.7 Close Project.

In many instances, government projects—and the priority accorded to them—result from public policy requirements, which stipulate that project managers ensure there is clear and continuing integration between these policy requirements, the program, and the project's scope and deliverables. Changes in policy might affect the program and, in turn, cause the project to be modified or even terminated.

4.1 Develop Project Charter

See Section 4.1 of the *PMBOK® Guide*—Third Edition.

4.1.1 Develop Project Charter: Inputs

See Section 4.1.1 of the *PMBOK® Guide*—Third Edition.

Government projects may be initiated in order to achieve a specific policy goal of the administration, for example, a reduction in budget deficit, or to achieve an essentially political goal, such as the nationalization or privatization of a utility company. However, the more common reasons to initiate a public sector project are:

- Public health needs (such as mass immunization, hospitals, sanitation, water purification, research, and food and pharmaceutical administration)
- Public safety needs (such as defense, counterterrorism, police and fire protection, disaster prevention and mitigation, crime prevention, land mine eradication, and drug trafficking control)

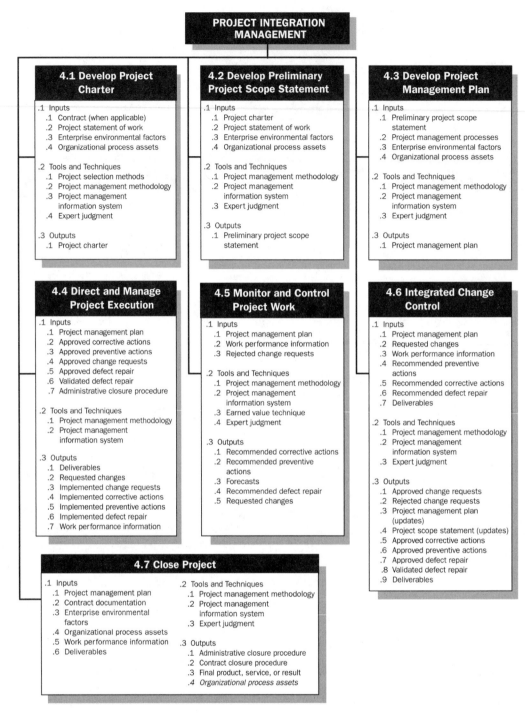

Figure 4-1. Project Integration Management

- Welfare, socioeconomic, and environmental needs (such as community development, poverty alleviation, education and schools, water supply, transportation and roads, energy, social security, environmental protection, and parks and recreation).

4.1.2 Develop Project Charter: Tools and Techniques

See Section 4.1.2 of the *PMBOK® Guide*—Third Edition.

4.1.3 Develop Project Charter: Outputs

See Section 4.1.3 of the *PMBOK® Guide*—Third Edition.

4.2 Develop Preliminary Project Scope Statement

See Section 4.2 of the *PMBOK® Guide*—Third Edition.

4.3 Develop Project Management Plan

See Section 4.3 of the *PMBOK® Guide*—Third Edition.

4.4 Direct and Manage Project Execution

See Section 4.4 of the *PMBOK® Guide*—Third Edition.

4.5 Monitor and Control Project Work

See Section 4.5 of the *PMBOK® Guide*—Third Edition.

4.6 Integrated Change Control

See Section 4.6 of the *PMBOK® Guide*—Third Edition.

4.7 Close Project

See Section 4.7 of the *PMBOK® Guide*—Third Edition.

4.7.1 Close Project: Inputs

See Section 4.7.1 of the *PMBOK® Guide*—Third Edition.

4.7.2 Close Project: Tools and Techniques

See Section 4.7.2 of the *PMBOK® Guide*—Third Edition.

4.7.3 Close Project: Outputs

See Section 4.7.3 of the *PMBOK® Guide*—Third Edition.

Sections 4.7.3.1 through 4.7.3.3 of the *PMBOK® Guide*—Third Edition discuss outputs from the Close Project process. An additional output specific to government projects is described below:

.4 **Organizational Process Assets.** See also section 4.7.3.4 of the *PMBOK® Guide*—Third Edition.

- *Project Files.* In government projects, the keeping of government records, including project files, is often required by a myriad of laws, regulations, and policies. The objective of these laws, regulations, and policies is to assure that project files may be accessed many years after completion of the project and understood by those unfamiliar with the project. The project files are maintained for the number of years prescribed by the laws, regulations, and policies applicable to the government body.

Chapter 5

Project Scope Management

See the introduction to Chapter 5 in the *PMBOK® Guide*—Third Edition.

5.1 Scope Planning

See Section 5.1 of the *PMBOK® Guide*—Third Edition, with the following additions to better express the scope planning ground rules that are unique to public sector projects.

Whether the organization is setting initial scope, revising the scope after the project is underway, or deciding whether to authorize the next phase, all government entities are subject to two overarching controls: spending authority and public accountability. When planning and executing scope, government entities are expressly prohibited by law from: *(a)* spending in excess of the approved budget without additional spending authority; *(b)* spending budgeted program funds on something other than that for which they were intended/budgeted; and *(c)* fraud, waste, and abuse of program funds (for instance, spending to meet budget levels so as to avoid losing the unspent funds). Discussion of these controls provides a good transition to other chapters dealing with specific areas of project control, such as cost and risk management.

5.1.1 Scope Planning: Inputs

See Section 5.1.1 of the *PMBOK® Guide*—Third Edition.

5.1.2 Scope Planning: Tools and Techniques

See Section 5.1.2 of the *PMBOK® Guide*—Third Edition.

5.1.3 Scope Planning: Outputs

See Section 5.1.3 of the *PMBOK® Guide*—Third Edition.

5.2 Scope Definition

See Section 5.2 of the *PMBOK® Guide*—Third Edition, with the recognition that government projects are faced with unique scope definition challenges in the context of

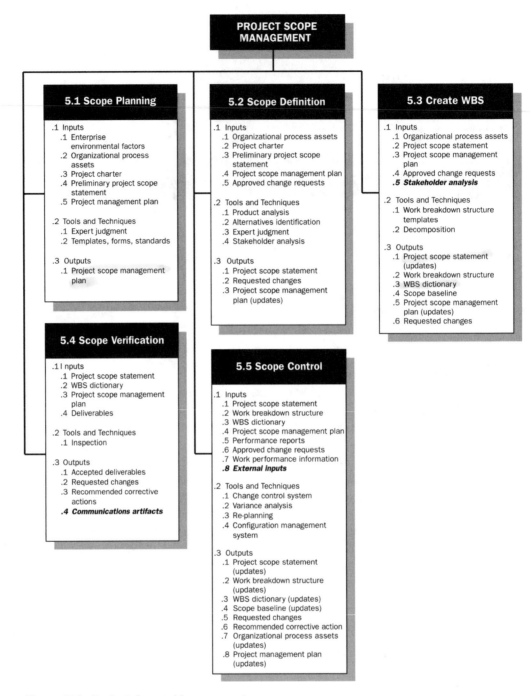

Figure 5-1. Project Scope Management

citizen-driven activity. Due to the presence of the general public as the ultimate stakeholder for government projects, the identification and conversion of stakeholders' needs into specific project requirements might become a never-ending task.

When addressing essential services like fire and police protection, utilities, etc., the public sector project scope must include a requirement of continuous service delivery throughout the project implementation.

For both new products and the enhancement of existing product initiatives, scope definition methods, such as packaging sets of desired changes in releases or phases, are primarily driven by political or social criteria (e.g., the need to implement a law change in an existing system by a certain date), not by efficiency factors (as is usually the case in the private sector).

5.2.1 Scope Definition: Inputs

See Section 5.2.1 of the *PMBOK® Guide*—Third Edition.

5.2.2 Scope Definition: Tools and Techniques

See Section 5.2.2 of the *PMBOK® Guide*—Third Edition.

5.2.3 Scope Definition: Outputs

See Section 5.2.3 of the *PMBOK® Guide*—Third Edition.

5.3 Create WBS

See Section 5.3 of the *PMBOK® Guide*—Third Edition.

5.3.1 Create WBS: Inputs

See Sections 5.3.1.1 through 5.3.1.4 of the *PMBOK® Guide*—Third Edition, with the addition of stakeholders' analysis (see Section 5.3.1.5) as a specific WBS input for government projects.

.5 Stakeholder Analysis

While not regularly an input on projects undertaken in the private sector, stakeholder analysis has a definite impact in the definition of work packages for public sector projects, due to hard boundaries between executing organizational stakeholders. It is not unusual for multiple ministries or agencies to execute a joint project, but, in most cases, this will result in separate project teams within each organization that will only coordinate activities through a few predefined communication channels. By contrast, in a private sector project, a similar issue would usually be resolved by creating a single, cross-functional project team based on efficiency criteria.

An additional consideration in a public sector project's WBS is the involvement of "opposition stakeholder" analysis. Involvement of opposition stakeholders in this early creation of the WBS may assist in a more "positive outcome" for all stakeholders. An additional consideration in public sector projects is the involvement of regulators, opposition stakeholders, the press, etc. (see Section 2.2) in the creation of the WBS and definition of work packages.

5.3.2 Create WBS: Tools and Techniques

See Section 5.3.2 of the *PMBOK® Guide*—Third Edition.

5.3.3 Create WBS: Outputs

See Section 5.3.3 of the *PMBOK® Guide*—Third Edition.

5.4 Scope Verification

Section 5.4 of the *PMBOK® Guide*—Third Edition describes Scope Verification as a stakeholders' verification and acceptance of the level of completion achieved by a project's deliverables. Since the ultimate stakeholder in a government project is the general public (which is not usually directly involved in the project), this verification is fulfilled through specific project controls such as compliance and public accountability. While each level of government may have unique characteristics, project controls that ensure governmental integrity are maintained across all public sector initiatives.

5.4.1 Scope Verification: Inputs

See Section 5.4.1 of the *PMBOK® Guide*—Third Edition.

5.4.2 Scope Verification: Tools and Techniques

See Section 5.4.2 of the *PMBOK® Guide*—Third Edition.

5.4.3 Scope Verification: Outputs

See Sections 5.4.3.1 to 5.4.3.3 of the *PMBOK® Guide*—Third Edition, with the addition of communication artifacts (Section 5.4.3.4):

.4 **Communication Artifacts**
While project communications are mostly handled under communications management as described in Chapter 10 of the *PMBOK® Guide*—Third Edition, scope verification can generate unplanned information flow, mostly external to the project. Governmental, parliamentary or public inquiries, audits and reviews (e.g., complaint-based or auto-initiated), and inspections from external funding organizations (e.g., World Bank, IMF, aid-giving countries, etc.) generate a variety of project reports, public communications, news conferences, mass-media interviews, and other communication artifacts not usually created during a private sector project.

5.5 Scope Control

See Section 5.5 of the *PMBOK® Guide*—Third Edition, with the recognition that governmental projects are more exposed to external influences (e.g., political disturbances, program-level impacts, etc.) depending upon circumstances outside a project's sphere of control or influence. Scope is always subject to change based on various influences—most of them sociopolitical—and these changes are usually reflected through budget adjustments based on priorities of the current political agenda.

5.5.1 Scope Control: Inputs

See Sections 5.5.1.1 to 5.5.1.7 of the *PMBOK® Guide*—Third Edition, with the addition of external inputs (Section 5.5.1.8):

.8 External Inputs

Government projects are often subject to external scope control inputs, such as approvals of project scope and scope changes from authorities, external funding requirements, and conditions that may be attached to the allocated budget.

5.5.2 Scope Control: Tools and Techniques

See Section 5.5.2 of the *PMBOK® Guide*—Third Edition.

5.5.3 Scope Control: Outputs

See Section 5.5.3 of the *PMBOK® Guide*—Third Edition.

Chapter 6

Project Time Management

See the introduction to Chapter 6 in the *PMBOK® Guide*—Third Edition.

6.1 Activity Definition

See Section 6.1 of the *PMBOK® Guide*—Third Edition.

6.2 Activity Sequencing

See Section 6.2 of the *PMBOK® Guide*—Third Edition.

6.3 Activity Resource Estimating

See Section 6.3 of the *PMBOK® Guide*—Third Edition.

6.4 Activity Duration Estimating

See Section 6.4 of the *PMBOK® Guide*—Third Edition.

6.4.1 Activity Duration Estimating: Inputs

See Sections 6.4.1.1 through 6.4.1.5 of the *PMBOK® Guide*—Third Edition.

.6 **Activity Resource Requirements**
In government projects, the availability of skilled human resources (see Section 9.1.1.1 of this document) or other resources may be impacted by preference laws (see Section 12.4.2.8 of this document).
See Sections 6.4.1.1 through 6.4.1.8 of the *PMBOK® Guide*—Third Edition.

6.4.2 Activity Duration Estimating: Tools and Techniques

See Section 6.4.2 of the *PMBOK® Guide*—Third Edition.

PROJECT TIME MANAGEMENT

6.1 Activity Definition

.1 Inputs
  .1 Enterprise environmental factors
  .2 Organizational process assets
  .3 Project scope statement
  .4 Work breakdown structure
  .5 WBS dictionary
  .6 Project management plan

.2 Tools and Techniques
  .1 Decomposition
  .2 Templates
  .3 Rolling wave planning
  .4 Expert judgment
  .5 Planning component

.3 Outputs
  .1 Activity list
  .2 Activity attributes
  .3 Milestone list
  .4 Requested changes

6.2 Activity Sequencing

.1 Inputs
  .1 Project scope statement
  .2 Activity list
  .3 Activity attributes
  .4 Milestone list
  .5 Approved change requests

.2 Tools and Techniques
  .1 Precedence Diagramming Method (PDM)
  .2 Arrow Diagramming Method (ADM)
  .3 Schedule network templates
  .4 Dependency determination
  .5 Applying leads and lags

.3 Outputs
  .1 Project schedule network diagrams
  .2 Activity list (updates)
  .3 Activity attributes (updates)
  .4 Requested changes

6.3 Activity Resource Estimating

.1 Inputs
  .1 Enterprise environmental factors
  .2 Organizational process assets
  .3 Activity list
  .4 Activity attributes
  .5 Resouce availability
  .6 Project management plan

.2 Tools and Techniques
  .1 Expert judgment
  .2 Alternatives analysis
  .3 Published estimating data
  .4 Project management software
  .5 Bottom-up estimating

.3 Outputs
  .1 Activity resource requirements
  .2 Activity attributes (updates)
  .3 Resource breakdown structure
  .4 Resource calendar (updates)
  .5 Requested changes

6.4 Activity Duration Estimating

.1 Inputs
  .1 Enterprise environmental factors
  .2 Organizational process assets
  .3 Project scope statement
  .4 Activity list
  .5 Activity attributes
  .6 *Activity resource requirements*
  .7 Resource calendar
  .8 Project management plan
     · Risk register
     · Activity cost estimates

.2 Tools and Techniques
  .1 Expert judgment
  .2 Analogous estimating
  .3 Parametric estimating
  .4 Three-point estimates
  .5 Reserve analysis

.3 Outputs
  .1 Activity duration estimates
  .2 Activity attributes (updates)

6.5 Schedule Development

.1 Inputs
  .1 Organizational process assets
  .2 *Project scope statement*
  .3 Activity list
  .4 Activity attributes
  .5 Project schedule network diagrams
  .6 Activity resource requirements
  .7 Resource calendars
  .8 Activity duration estimates
  .9 Project management plan
     · Risk register
  .10 Line-item projects

.2 Tools and Techniques
  .1 Schedule network analysis
  .2 Critical path method
  .3 Schedule compression
  .4 What-if scenario analysis
  .5 Resource leveling
  .6 Critical chain method
  .7 Project management software
  .8 Applying calendars
  .9 Adjusting leads and lags
  .10 Schedule model
  .11 Obligations

.3 Outputs
  .1 Project schedule
  .2 Schedule model data
  .3 Schedule baseline
  .4 Resource requirements (updates)
  .5 Activity attributes (updates)
  .6 Project calendar (updates)
  .7 Requested changes
  .8 Project management plan (updates)
     · Schedule management plan (updates)

6.6 Schedule Control

.1 Inputs
  .1 Schedule management plan
  .2 Schedule baseline
  .3 Performance reports
  .4 Approved change requests

.2 Tools and Techniques
  .1 Progress reporting
  .2 Schedule change control system
  .3 Performance measurement
  .4 Project management software
  .5 Variance analysis
  .6 Schedule comparison bar charts

.3 Outputs
  .1 Schedule model data (updates)
  .2 Schedule baseline (updates)
  .3 Performance measurements
  .4 Requested changes
  .5 Recommended corrective actions
  .6 Organizational process assets (updates)
  .7 Activity list (updates)
  .8 Activity attributes (updates)
  .9 Project management plan (updates)

Figure 6-1. Project Time Management

6.4.3 Activity Duration Estimating: Outputs
See Section 6.4.3 of the *PMBOK® Guide*—Third Edition.

6.5 Schedule Development
See Section 6.5 of the *PMBOK® Guide*—Third Edition.

6.5.1 Schedule Development: Inputs

.1 Organizational Process Assets
See Section 6.5.1.1 of the *PMBOK® Guide*—Third Edition.

.2 Project Scope Statement
In addition to the inputs described in Section 6.5.1.2 of the *PMBOK® Guide*—Third Edition, the annual budget cycle is a unique, and often most difficult, constraint for government projects. Budgets are typically for one fiscal year at a time. This means that projects and programs often must be divided into one-year slices. Use it or lose it provisions generally require funds to be spent by the end of the fiscal year. Project delays can cause the loss of funding if work moves from one fiscal year into the next. Fortunately, funds are generally appropriated to programs rather than individual projects (see Section 1.6 of this document). Effective program managers can often move funds between projects to minimize the overall loss of funding. However, some very large projects keep their budgetary identity. No movement of funds to or from one of these projects can be processed without clearance by the government or those to whom the government has delegated that authority.

.3 Activity List
See Section 6.5.1.3 of the *PMBOK® Guide*—Third Edition.

.4 Activity Attributes
See Section 6.5.1.4 of the *PMBOK® Guide*—Third Edition.

.5 Project Schedule Network Diagrams
See Section 6.5.1.5 of the *PMBOK® Guide*—Third Edition.

.6 Activity Resource Requirements
See Section 6.5.1.6 of the *PMBOK® Guide*—Third Edition.

.7 Resource Calendars
See Section 6.5.1.7 of the *PMBOK® Guide*—Third Edition.

.8 Activity Duration Estimates
See Section 6.5.1.8 of the *PMBOK® Guide*—Third Edition.

.9 Project Management Plan
See Section 6.5.1.9 of the *PMBOK® Guide*—Third Edition.

.10 Line-Item Projects
These projects are added to the budget by the representative body on a project-

by-project basis. They often are not supported by a proposal from the executive (see Section 2.1.2). The representatives set their schedules and budget. As a result, these projects may have poorly defined scopes, inadequate funding, or unreasonable schedules. The project manager must work with the customer expeditiously to determine the scope of work and the appropriate acquisition strategy to accomplish the project within the time constraints.

6.5.2 Schedule Development: Tools and Techniques

See Sections 6.5.2.1 through 6.5.2.10 of the *PMBOK® Guide*—Third Edition.

In addition to these tools and techniques, another, which is common in government projects, is described below:

.11 Obligations

Obligations or encumbrances help to address the annual budget cycle constraint (see Section 6.5.1.2). They are useful on projects with large procurements, but can be used only if the representative body enacts rules to make them possible. Some governments can obligate the funds if they are contractually committed before the end of the fiscal year. An obligation places the contract funds into a separate account that can be used only for the specific contract. The funds remain available for additional years, depending upon the rules set by the government body. This technique avoids the need to appropriate funds in each fiscal year. Obligations are also used in intergovernmental agreements, sometimes called government transfer payments.

6.5.3 Schedule Development: Outputs

See Section 6.5.3 of the *PMBOK® Guide*—Third Edition.

6.6 Schedule Control

See Section 6.6 of the *PMBOK® Guide*—Third Edition.

Chapter 7

Project Cost Management

The *PMBOK® Guide*—Third Edition defines Project Cost Management as "the processes involved in planning, estimating, budgeting, and controlling so that the project can be completed within the approved budget." Chapter 7 of the *PMBOK® Guide*—Third Edition describes three processes:

7.1 Cost Estimating
7.2 Cost Budgeting
7.3 Cost Control

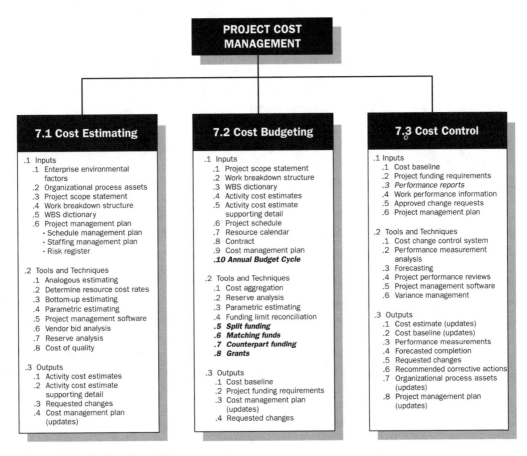

Figure 7-1. Project Cost Management

7.1 Cost Estimating

See Section 7.1 of the *PMBOK® Guide*—Third Edition.

7.2 Cost Budgeting

As stated in the *PMBOK® Guide*—Third Edition, "Cost budgeting involves aggregating the estimated costs of individual schedule activities or work packages to establish a total cost baseline for measuring project performance."

7.2.1 Cost Budgeting: Inputs

Section 7.2.1 of the *PMBOK® Guide*—Third Edition discusses nine inputs to Cost Budgeting (See 7.2.1.1 through 7.2.1.9), all of which are used on government projects. There is an additional input used when managing government projects, the "annual budget cycle."

.10 Annual Budget Cycle

The annual budget cycle is the unique, and often most difficult, time constraint for government projects. To prevent abuse, the governing body budgets funds for only a limited time. Budgets are typically for one fiscal year at a time. This means that projects and programs may be divided into one-year slices. "Use it or lose it" provisions require funds to be spent by the end of the fiscal year. Project delays can cause the loss of funding if work moves from one fiscal year into the next. Fortunately, funds are generally appropriated to programs rather than individual projects. Effective program managers can often move funds between projects to minimize the overall loss of funding.

7.2.2 Cost Budgeting: Tools and Techniques

The *PMBOK® Guide*—Third Edition describes four tools and techniques (see 7.2.2.1 through 7.2.2.4). There are five additional tools used in government projects:

.5 Split Funding

If a single project receives financial contributions from more than one program or fiscal year, it is *split-funded*. Common methods of split funding include *defined elements of work, defined contribution*, and *percentage split.*

Split funding by program. Programs are discussed in Section 1.6 of this standard. Government bodies in large governments generally assign funds to programs rather than to individual projects. They set rules for how the funds are to be divided among individual projects. If the government body budgets by program, each project must be funded from one or more of these programs. It is possible that a single project can contribute to the goals of more than one program. This is particularly common in transportation infrastructure projects. For example, a road-widening project could be combined with pavement rehabilitation, bridge rehabilitation, seismic retrofit, or new signals. These are generally budgeted as separate programs. Similar situations are common whenever new facilities are budgeted separately from rehabilitation. It generally makes sense to have a single contractor perform both the new work and the rehabilitation at a particular location. This minimizes the overhead cost of developing and managing multiple contracts, and it minimizes the disruption to the occupants of the facility.

To the legislative body, *defined elements of work* is often the preferred method, because each program pays only for the elements that it wants. However, this method requires a detailed manual accounting system, because an automated system can seldom discern which elements are being worked on. Such a manual process is prone to inaccuracy, and requires a large commitment of time for reporting and auditing. The increased cost generally outweighs the slight increase in the accuracy of charges. The *defined elements of work* method also requires a far more detailed work breakdown structure (WBS) than the other two methods. To capture each program's portion accurately, the WBS must be defined to a level where each program's portion maps uniquely to a set of WBS elements. This level of detail is generally far greater than what is needed to manage the project. The *defined contribution* does not require an amendment to the WBS. Typically, contributions are established as a *percentage split*. When the limit is reached for the fixed programs, the split is changed to a 100 percent payment by the risk-bearing program. If the project is completed within budget, the change never occurs. *Percentage split* is the simplest approach and is often the most efficient method. The contribution of each program is estimated at the start of the project. Based on that estimate, each program bears its percentage of the project cost. Since programs fund many projects, variances on one project will probably be counterbalanced by opposite variances on other projects.

Split funding by fiscal year. Split funding by fiscal year is funding allocated over more than one annual budget cycle. (The annual budget cycle is discussed in Section 7.2.1.) If a project begins in one fiscal year and ends in another, it will need funding from the budget of each fiscal year in which there is project work. This split funding by fiscal year can be decreased through *obligations*, if the government body allows them (see Section 6.4.2.). Funding by fiscal year requires that project managers plan their work by fiscal year with great care. This is particularly true in large governments with many levels of review. In the United States government, for instance, the President submits a budget to Congress in January for the fiscal year that begins in October. Before this, the executive staff must assemble all the supporting data for the budget. Staff must also agree on priorities for the allocation of limited funds. To be included in the January budget, the project manager must have project plans completed by 30 June of the previous year. This is more than fifteen months before the start of the fiscal year. Once a budget request is submitted, changes are difficult to effect. Fortunately, funds are generally appropriated to programs rather than individual projects (see Section 1.6). Program managers can use funds from projects that underrun their fiscal year budgets to fund the overruns in other projects. These are *fiscal year* variances, not variances in the total cost of the project. Private sector firms could not survive with the government budget process. They must respond quickly to market challenges from their competitors. Without a quick response, they will lose business and may descend into bankruptcy. Large private firms, therefore, delegate the detailed budget decisions to smaller cost centers. The manager of each cost center has clear performance measures: make a profit, satisfy customers so that the firm gets return business, and obey the law. In government, there is no profit motive and customers seldom have the option not to return. Paradoxically, fiscal year funding can have an effect that is opposite to what is intended. Annual budgets are intended to establish limits on the executive. In *operational work,* annual budgets achieve this goal; in projects, they often fail. For a discussion of operations and projects, see Section 1.2.2 of the *PMBOK® Guide*—Third Edition.

The executive must request budgets for each project in fiscal year slices. This focus on fiscal years can draw attention away from the overall multiyear cost of the project. The government body may not see this overall cost. Projects can incur large overall cost overruns without the government body becoming aware of this fact. Therefore, government bodies need to be aware of this problem and require multiyear reports. Project managers should provide multiyear reports to their project sponsors. Government accounting standards often fail to recognize the peculiar needs of multiyear projects. Project managers should keep records on the entire project that are reconciled with the government's official accounts. Some governments have begun to adopt performance-based budgeting as an alternative to the rigid annual budget process. This is discussed in Section 8.1.2.

.6 Matching Funds

Matching funds are a form of split funding by program (see Section 7.2.2.5). When governments "devolve" project selection to lower government bodies, they often require those lower bodies to pay a portion of the project costs. This ensures that the lower government is committed to the project. Matching funds may be apportioned on a percentage basis or as a defined contribution.

.7 Obligations

Obligations are tools to minimize the impact of split funding by fiscal year. They can be used only where there is a contractual commitment to fund the project. For more discussion on obligations, see Section 6.5.2.11 of this document.

.8 Counterpart Funding

This is also called "counterfunding." This tool involves funding from the private sector, and is an option in "developing" countries, which will not have enough funds for many years to meet all the basic infrastructure needs of their population.

.9 Grants

Grants are tools used to acquire additional funding for projects. Grant cycles and amounts vary. Grants have required application specifications and deadlines that must be met.

7.2.3 Cost Budgeting: Outputs

See Section 7.2.3 of the *PMBOK® Guide*—Third Edition.

7.3 Cost Control

See Section 7.3 of the *PMBOK® Guide*—Third Edition.

7.3.1 Cost Control: Inputs

Section 7.3.1.3 of the *PMBOK® Guide*—Third Edition identifies performance reports as an input to cost control. Performance reports are also cost control inputs for government projects. These reports are not only internal to the organization, but they provide project performance information to external funding sources. Upon acceptance of the project performance reports, the external funding sources release funds to the project. These reports are distributed to the external stakeholders by the government body.

7.3.2 Cost Control: Tools and Techniques

See Section 7.3.2 of the *PMBOK® Guide*—Third Edition.

7.3.3 Cost Control: Outputs

See Section 7.3.3 of the *PMBOK® Guide*—Third Edition.

Chapter 8

Project Quality Management

The *PMBOK® Guide*—Third Edition states on page 179 that "Project Quality Management processes include all the activities of the performing organization that determine quality policies, objectives, and responsibilities so that the project will satisfy the needs for which it was undertaken." On government projects, these needs are defined by the government body acting on behalf of the public. In large governments, the needs are generally stated as goals for a program, rather than for individual projects. Project Quality Management on government projects is frequently an oversight activity undertaken as part of procurement; see Chapter 12 (Project Procurement Management) in this extension.

Chapter 8 of the *PMBOK® Guide*—Third Edition describes three processes:

8.1 **Quality Planning**
8.2 **Perform Quality Assurance**
8.3 **Perform Quality Control**

8.1 Quality Planning

8.1.1 Quality Planning: Inputs

Section 8.1.1 of the *PMBOK® Guide*—Third Edition discusses inputs to Quality Planning. All inputs listed are used on government projects, and two have particular application in government:

.1 **Enterprise Environmental Factors**
Governmental agency regulations, rules, standards, and guidelines specific to the application area may affect the project. This is particularly true in developing the project charter, and all of the organization's enterprise environmental factors and systems that surround and influence the project's success. See also Section 4.1.1.3 of the *PMBOK® Guide*—Third Edition.

.2 **Organizational Process Assets**
According to the *PMBOK® Guide*—Third Edition, "the quality policy, as endorsed by senior management, is the intended direction of a performing organization with regard to quality." In government, quality policy is rooted in the laws and

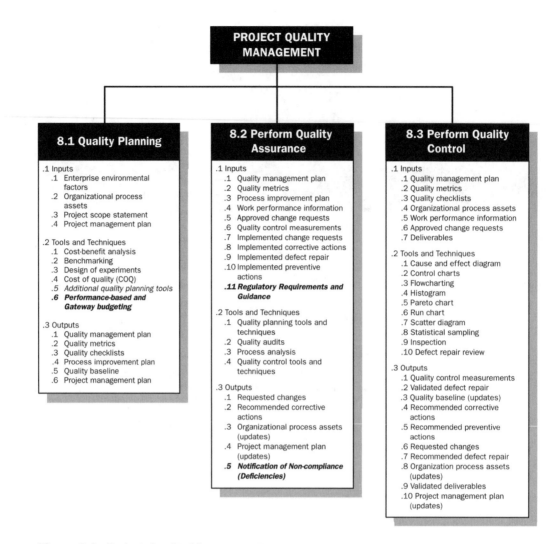

PROJECT QUALITY MANAGEMENT

8.1 Quality Planning

.1 Inputs
  .1 Enterprise environmental factors
  .2 Organizational process assets
  .3 Project scope statement
  .4 Project management plan

.2 Tools and Techniques
  .1 Cost-benefit analysis
  .2 Benchmarking
  .3 Design of experiments
  .4 Cost of quality (COQ)
  .5 *Additional quality planning tools*
  .6 Performance-based and Gateway budgeting

.3 Outputs
  .1 Quality management plan
  .2 Quality metrics
  .3 Quality checklists
  .4 Process improvement plan
  .5 Quality baseline
  .6 Project management plan

8.2 Perform Quality Assurance

.1 Inputs
  .1 Quality management plan
  .2 Quality metrics
  .3 Process improvement plan
  .4 Work performance information
  .5 Approved change requests
  .6 Quality control measurements
  .7 Implemented change requests
  .8 Implemented corrective actions
  .9 Implemented defect repair
  .10 Implemented preventive actions
  .11 Regulatory Requirements and Guidance

.2 Tools and Techniques
  .1 Quality planning tools and techniques
  .2 Quality audits
  .3 Process analysis
  .4 Quality control tools and techniques

.3 Outputs
  .1 Requested changes
  .2 Recommended corrective actions
  .3 Organizational process assets (updates)
  .4 Project management plan (updates)
  .5 Notification of Non-compliance (Deficiencies)

8.3 Perform Quality Control

.1 Inputs
  .1 Quality management plan
  .2 Quality metrics
  .3 Quality checklists
  .4 Organizational process assets
  .5 Work performance information
  .6 Approved change requests
  .7 Deliverables

.2 Tools and Techniques
  .1 Cause and effect diagram
  .2 Control charts
  .3 Flowcharting
  .4 Histogram
  .5 Pareto chart
  .6 Run chart
  .7 Scatter diagram
  .8 Statistical sampling
  .9 Inspection
  .10 Defect repair review

.3 Outputs
  .1 Quality control measurements
  .2 Validated defect repair
  .3 Quality baseline (updates)
  .4 Recommended corrective actions
  .5 Recommended preventive actions
  .6 Requested changes
  .7 Recommended defect repair
  .8 Organization process assets (updates)
  .9 Validated deliverables
  .10 Project management plan (updates)

Figure 8-1. Project Quality Management

regulations, or in policies established by the government body. If quality policy is established in the laws and regulations, the government body will generally add further details in rules and procedures.

The *PMBOK® Guide*—Third Edition also states on page 184, "the project management team is responsible for ensuring that the project stakeholders are fully aware of [the quality policy]." On government projects, this means that they must be aware of their responsibilities under the constitution and under law; see Section 1.2.4 on (Why are Government Projects Unique?).

Because government quality policy is rooted in the constitution and other documents that seldom change, government quality policies should not change much. Projects may vary considerably, but they remain focused on service to the voters and taxpayers in accordance with established quality policy.

.3 Project Scope Statement

See Section 8.1.1.3 of the *PMBOK® Guide*—Third Edition.

.4 Project Management Plan

See Section 8.1.1.4 of the *PMBOK® Guide*—Third Edition.

8.1.2 Quality Planning: Tools and Techniques

Section 8.1.2 of the *PMBOK® Guide*—Third Edition discusses five tools and techniques for Quality Planning. All are used on government projects. Under the fifth heading, an additional tool specific to government projects is mentioned:

.1 Cost-Benefit Analysis

See Section 8.1.2.1 of the *PMBOK® Guide*—Third Edition.

.2 Benchmarking

See Section 8.1.2.2 of the *PMBOK® Guide*—Third Edition.

.3 Design of Experiments

See Section 8.1.2.3 of the *PMBOK® Guide*—Third Edition.

.4 Cost of Quality

See Section 8.1.2.4 of the *PMBOK® Guide*—Third Edition.

.5 Additional Quality Planning Tools

See Section 8.1.2.5 of the *PMBOK® Guide*—Third Edition. One additional quality-planning tool is performance-based budgeting; see Section 7.2 of this document.

.6 Performance-Based and Gateway Budgeting

Sections 6.4.1.6, 7.3.1.5, and 7.3.2.4 of this document discuss the problems of the annual budget cycle. Some governments have begun to adopt performance-based budgeting as an alternative to the rigid annual process. For projects, this is rooted in the concept of the "*triple constraint*" (see Section 1.3 of the *PMBOK® Guide*—Third Edition).

Quality projects deliver the required product scope on time and within budget. If a change is made to any of the three factors, at least one other factor must change. Every change is, therefore, a change in quality.

For programs and projects, the government body establishes performance measures for each of the three quality factors. Program managers are permitted to trade off between the three factors to achieve the overall program goals. This includes permission to change the annual budget, within prescribed limits.

Performance-based budgeting can be of great benefit to the voters and taxpayers. However, there are pitfalls:

- Performance measures must be carefully designed to encourage desirable behavior.
- Poorly defined measures can require managers to make the wrong decisions in order to meet their performance target.
- The design of the measures requires a thorough understanding of the program.

In large governments, the executive generally reports progress to the government body only once a year. It would be wasteful to gather the data for more frequent reports, and the legislative cycle typically allows the government body to take action only on an annual cycle.

For performance-based budgeting, annual reports are inadequate. If performance is not adequate or the process is abused, the government body must be able to take action more frequently than once a year. This typically requires an independent "watchdog" body, with paid auditors who review data from the program and report to the government body if there is a need to take immediate action.

Other governmental entities are employing "gateway" or "zero-balance" budgeting. Considering the three factors of project management (scope, time, and cost), these entities begin with a "zero-balance" budget at the start of the project, ask the project manager to determine the cost of the project in phases, and request these monies prior to the beginning of a new phase. Gateways are appropriate windows in the project process for monitoring progress and making decisions through project reviews. The following gateways are suggested for budgeting considerations:

(a) Phase 1—Concept
- Initial gateway budget request
- Project proposal for budget support/selection
- Initial negotiations with customer/stakeholders
- Initial staffing of project team, project manager selected, project team leads identified, core team members selected
- Broad scope: product and professional services
- Complete identification of and staffing of project team.

(b) Phase 2—Definition
- Second gateway budget request
- Detailed scope
- Task list—tool used for project work breakdown structure development
- Project work breakdown structure—tool used for gateway identification and utilization
- Risk analysis.

(c) Phase 3—Design and Implementation
- Design of final product
- Implementation plan—implementation of product design
- Installation or conduct of project activities
- Delivery of services.

(d) Phase 4—Project Closeout and Follow-up
- Customer/stakeholder feedback
- Financial performance
- Project documentation
- Lessons learned
- Closeout.

The gateways are usually identified by selecting a small group from a highly detailed work breakdown structure (WBS) diagram, where each WBS spans no less than 80 hours. This allows the project manager to "track" resource loading. The project manager can then prepare and submit a new budgeting request within the time frame necessary to keep the project funded over the next budgeting period. In effect, gateway or zero-balancing budgeting assists the project manager in better understanding the cost benefit of each phase of the project, and making the calculations for earned value more meaningful to the sponsors and stakeholders.

8.1.3 Quality Planning: Outputs

See Section 8.1.3 of the *PMBOK® Guide*—Third Edition.

8.2 Perform Quality Assurance

Quality assurance, for some government-regulated facilities, such as facilities for creating electricity using nuclear materials, facilities for handling transuranics or special nuclear materials, hazardous waste disposal sites, drinking water purification facilities, etc., is substantially different from the norm for other industries, as specified in the *PMBOK® Guide*—Third Edition. Such facilities must meet specific requirements and regulations, as well as the supporting guidance documents that are often issued by agencies overseeing these facilities. The government is ultimately responsible for quality assurance, a duty that cannot be delegated.

8.2.1 Perform Quality Assurance: Inputs

Section 8.2.1 of the *PMBOK® Guide*—Third Edition describes ten inputs to Perform Quality Assurance, all of which apply in government projects. An eleventh input, Regulatory Requirements and Guidance, has been added, and its special application to government projects is explained in Section 8.2.1.11.

.1 **Quality Management Plan**
See Section 8.2.1.1 of the *PMBOK® Guide*—Third Edition.

.2 **Quality Metrics**
See Section 8.2.1.2 of the *PMBOK® Guide*—Third Edition.

.3 **Process Improvement Plan**
See Section 8.2.1.3 of the *PMBOK® Guide*—Third Edition.

.4 **Work Performance Information**
See Section 8.2.1.4 of the *PMBOK® Guide*—Third Edition.

.5 **Approved Change Requests**
See Section 8.2.1.5 of the *PMBOK® Guide*—Third Edition.

.6 **Quality Control Measurements**
See Section 8.2.1.6 of the *PMBOK® Guide*—Third Edition.

.7 **Implemented Change Requests**
See Section 8.2.1.7 of the *PMBOK® Guide*—Third Edition.

.8 **Implemented Corrective Actions**
See Section 8.2.1.8 of the *PMBOK® Guide*—Third Edition.

.9 **Implemented Defect Repair**
See Section 8.2.1.9 of the *PMBOK® Guide*—Third Edition.

.10 **Implemented Preventive Actions**
See Section 8.2.1.10 of the *PMBOK® Guide*—Third Edition.

.11 Regulatory Requirements and Guidance

This heading refers to regulatory requirements and guidance, such as that expressed in national, regional, and local regulations, as well as documents produced by standards-setting organizations like PMI, ISO, and others. These provide a level of work guidance for audits, surveillance, testing, and inspections. The results of audits, surveillance, testing, and inspections should be formally documented and included in the overall Quality Assurance process.

8.2.2 Perform Quality Assurance: Tools and Techniques

.1 Quality Planning Tools and Techniques

See Section 8.2.2.1 of the *PMBOK® Guide*—Third Edition.

.2 Quality Audits

Additional aspects of quality audits are inspections, surveillance, and walkthroughs. The inspections and surveillance are also structured, independent reviews, but are more in-line with performance-based activities checks than reviews to determine whether project activities are in compliance. The walkthrough is a process during which a trained specialist observes activities based on procedure compliance, where the activity is being walked through, not performed. In this instance, quality audits inaccuracies can be observed, recorded and remedied without the hazard of non-compliance.

.3 Process Analysis

See Section 8.2.2.3 of the *PMBOK® Guide*—Third Edition.

.4 Quality Control Tools and Techniques

See Section 8.2.2.4 of the *PMBOK® Guide*—Third Edition.

8.2.3 Perform Quality Assurance: Outputs

Section 8.2.3 of the *PMBOK® Guide*—Third Edition describes four outputs of Perform Quality Assurance, all of which apply in government projects. A fifth output of importance in government work ("Notification of Non-Compliance [Deficiencies]") appears in this extension as Section 8.2.3.5.

.1 Requested Changes

See Section 8.2.3.1 of the *PMBOK® Guide*—Third Edition.

.2 Recommended Corrective Actions

See Section 8.2.3.2 of the *PMBOK® Guide*—Third Edition.

.3 Organizational Process Assets (Updates)

See Section 8.2.3.3 of the *PMBOK® Guide*—Third Edition.

.4 Project Management Plan (Updates)

See Section 8.2.3.4 of the *PMBOK® Guide*—Third Edition.

.5 Notification of Non-Compliance (Deficiencies)

Continuous quality improvement also relies on observing Quality Assurance inaccuracies during audits, inspections, surveillance, and walk-throughs. When quality issues arise, such as non-compliance with a requirement or a violation of regulatory requirements, state or plan procedures, documentation is required that details these issues, including the requirement in question and the item(s) of non-compliance. Tracking these items of non-compliance from the time of observation to closeout and detailing the corrective actions taken as "lessons learned" can assist in preventing additional non-compliance.

8.3 Perform Quality Control

See Section 8.3 of the *PMBOK® Guide*—Third Edition.

Chapter 9

Project Human Resource Management

According to the *PMBOK® Guide*—Third Edition, "Project Human Resource Management includes the processes that organize and manage the project team." Project Human Resource Management is one of the two Project Management Knowledge Areas in the *PMBOK® Guide*—Third Edition that focus on the acquisition and use of project resources. The other is Project Procurement Management (see the introduction to Chapter 12). Human resources used on a project are obtained either from inside the performing organization or they are obtained by procurement. Human resources used on a project fall into the following categories:

- Human resources obtained from outside the performing organization—discussed in both Chapters 9 and 12
- Human resources obtained from within the performing organization—discussed only in Chapter 9.

Chapter 9 of the *PMBOK® Guide*—Third Edition describes four processes involved in Project Human Resource Management:

9.1 Human Resource Planning
9.2 Acquire Project Team
9.3 Develop Project Team
9.4 Manage Project Team

9.1 Human Resource Planning

See Section 9.1 of the *PMBOK® Guide*—Third Edition.

9.1.1 Human Resource Planning: Inputs

Section 9.1.1 of the *PMBOK® Guide*—Third Edition discusses inputs to Human Resource Planning. Among the enterprise environmental factors and organizational process assets, additional factors have special application in government projects:

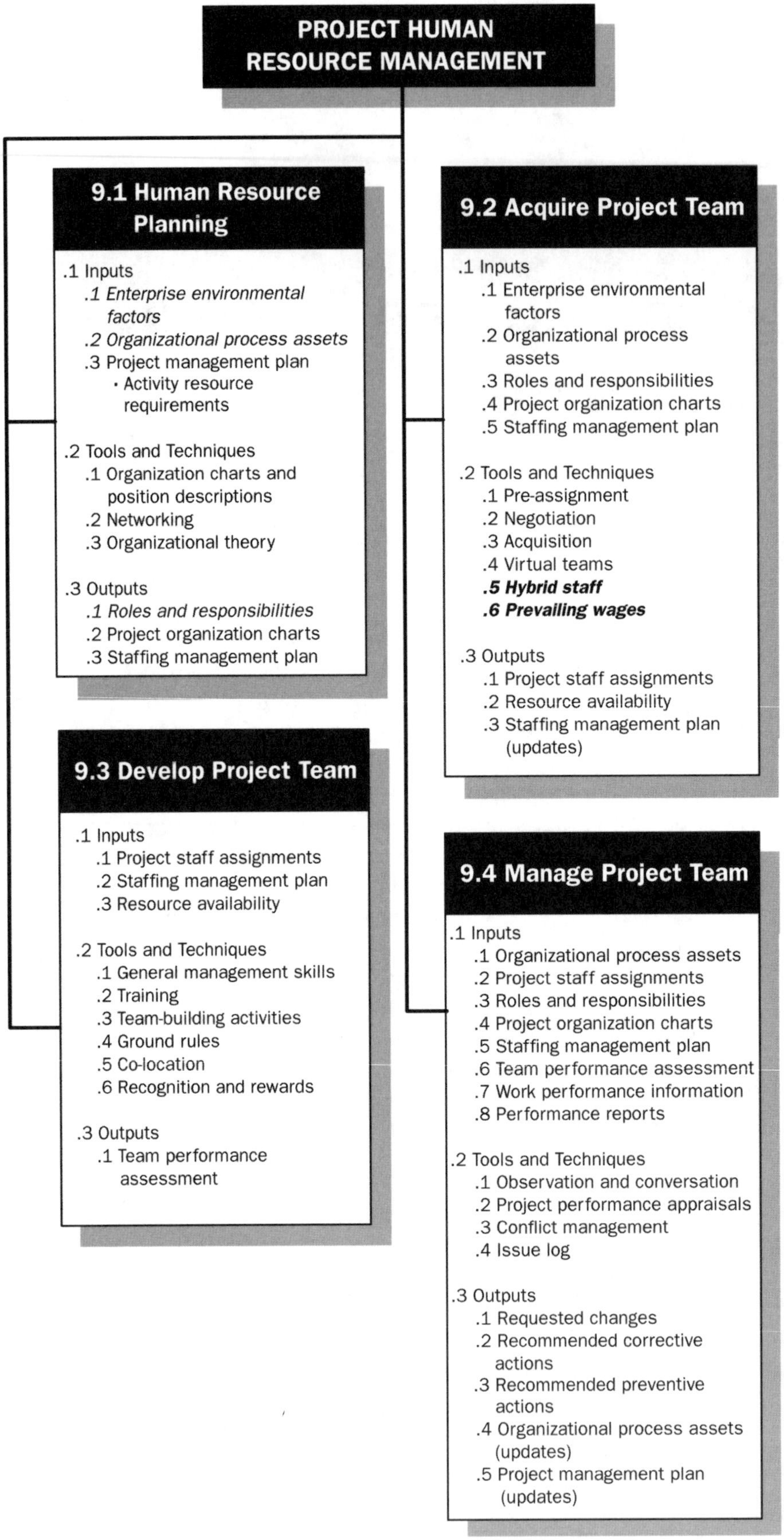

PROJECT HUMAN RESOURCE MANAGEMENT

9.1 Human Resource Planning

.1 Inputs
   .1 *Enterprise environmental factors*
   .2 *Organizational process assets*
   .3 Project management plan
      · Activity resource requirements

.2 Tools and Techniques
   .1 Organization charts and position descriptions
   .2 Networking
   .3 Organizational theory

.3 Outputs
   .1 *Roles and responsibilities*
   .2 Project organization charts
   .3 Staffing management plan

9.2 Acquire Project Team

.1 Inputs
   .1 Enterprise environmental factors
   .2 Organizational process assets
   .3 Roles and responsibilities
   .4 Project organization charts
   .5 Staffing management plan

.2 Tools and Techniques
   .1 Pre-assignment
   .2 Negotiation
   .3 Acquisition
   .4 Virtual teams
   .5 Hybrid staff
   .6 Prevailing wages

.3 Outputs
   .1 Project staff assignments
   .2 Resource availability
   .3 Staffing management plan (updates)

9.3 Develop Project Team

.1 Inputs
   .1 Project staff assignments
   .2 Staffing management plan
   .3 Resource availability

.2 Tools and Techniques
   .1 General management skills
   .2 Training
   .3 Team-building activities
   .4 Ground rules
   .5 Co-location
   .6 Recognition and rewards

.3 Outputs
   .1 Team performance assessment

9.4 Manage Project Team

.1 Inputs
   .1 Organizational process assets
   .2 Project staff assignments
   .3 Roles and responsibilities
   .4 Project organization charts
   .5 Staffing management plan
   .6 Team performance assessment
   .7 Work performance information
   .8 Performance reports

.2 Tools and Techniques
   .1 Observation and conversation
   .2 Project performance appraisals
   .3 Conflict management
   .4 Issue log

.3 Outputs
   .1 Requested changes
   .2 Recommended corrective actions
   .3 Recommended preventive actions
   .4 Organizational process assets (updates)
   .5 Project management plan (updates)

Figure 9-1. Project Human Resource Management

.1 Enterprise Environmental Factors

See Section 9.1.1 of the *PMBOK® Guide*—Third Edition for a discussion of the list of enterprise environmental factors. In addition to these factors, constraints limit the project team's options, including one constraint that is unique to government. Examples of constraints that can limit flexibility in the Human Resource Planning process are:

- **Organizational structure.** An organization whose basic structure is a weak matrix means a relatively weaker role for the project manager (Section 2.3.3). In government projects, the authority to make certain key decisions cannot be delegated to persons who are not government employees. For example, the selection of a seller to award a contract (Section 12.4) must be done by a government body or a duly authorized government employee.

- **Collective bargaining agreements.** See Section 9.1.1 of the *PMBOK® Guide*—Third Edition.

- **Economic conditions.** See Section 9.1.1 of the *PMBOK® Guide*—Third Edition.

- **Civil service system.** The civil service system distinguishes government human resource management from that in the private sector. In government, there is a likelihood that official policies will change from administration to another. Government employees must often implement policies that directly contradict those of a prior administration. In the past, this was often conducted through a "spoils system," where each new administration replaced government employees *en masse*. The spoils system has generally been replaced around the world by a merit-based civil service system. Civil servants hold office from one administration to another, but they must remain politically neutral. Regardless of these personal beliefs and values, civil servants are legally and ethically required to carry out the will of the citizens. In many nations, civil servants may not be members of political parties or engage in any political activity other than voting.

  As a guarantee of their neutrality, civil servants have tenure in their positions. Executives cannot remove a civil servant without demonstrating cause; this can become a significant issue in establishing a project team, since each civil servant's position must be preserved—and assigning a civil servant to a position perceived as inferior might be deemed a constructive demotion. Budget and law control civil service employee numbers. A project manager is not afforded the ability to hire personnel to fill critical skills needs (such as project controls) without going through a bureaucratic process. If a hiring is authorized, the process can take several months. Because project managers do not have the freedom to choose their staff, the project manager must create a viable, performing team from the available staff. Project managers need to master teambuilding skills, understand the different personality types, and motivate these individuals to produce a functioning team.

- **Preferences and restrictions.** Government bodies will often give employment preferences to particular population groups. These may be ethnic groups, people who are deemed to be disadvantaged (e.g., women and disabled people), people to whom others feel indebted (e.g., military veterans), or citizens. In addition, government bodies may place restrictions on employment based on security requirements (e.g., citizens only) (see also Section 12.1.2.4).

.2 Organizational Process Assets

- **Freedom of information.** Project managers might find themselves legally required to make public any notes taken at meetings in which appraisals of staff performance or interpersonal problems were discussed.
- **Privacy acts.** In most countries, government employees are bound by acts such as the privacy act, public service regulations, and public service act. These acts and regulations provide for the establishment and management of the public service, and implement provisions regulating the disclosure of information and code of conduct by public servants. The project manager needs to be familiar with the requirements stated in these acts and regulations of the country and locality, and ensure that they are followed.

.3 Project Management Plan

See Section 9.1.1.3 of *PMBOK® Guide*—Third Edition.

9.1.2 Human Resource Planning: Tools and Techniques

See Section 9.1.2 of the *PMBOK® Guide*—Third Edition.

9.1.3 Human Resource Planning: Outputs

Section 9.1.3 of the *PMBOK® Guide*—Third Edition discusses outputs from Human Resource Planning. Among the roles and responsibilities, one item has particular application in government projects.

.1 Roles and Responsibilities

See Section 9.1.3.1 of the *PMBOK® Guide*—Third Edition.

- **Authority.** In government projects, the authority to make certain key decisions may not be delegated to persons who are not government employees, which represents a constraint (Section 9.1.1.1 of this extension) on project staff assignments.
- See also Sections 9.1.3.2 and 9.1.3.3 of the *PMBOK® Guide*—Third Edition.

9.2 Acquire Project Team

See Section 9.2 of the *PMBOK® Guide*—Third Edition.

9.2.1 Acquire Project Team: Inputs

See Section 9.2.1 of the *PMBOK® Guide*—Third Edition.

9.2.2 Acquire Project Team: Tools and Techniques

Section 9.2.2 of the *PMBOK® Guide*—Third Edition discusses tools and techniques for staff acquisition. Two additional techniques also have application on government projects, one under Negotiation, and one in an added heading, hybrid staff.

.1 Pre-Assignment

See Section 9.2.2.1 of the *PMBOK® Guide*—Third Edition.

.2 Negotiation

See Section 9.2.2.2 of the *PMBOK® Guide*—Third Edition.

   Although it is seldom recognized in formal human resource systems, employees are frequently able to choose among government projects. The civil service system makes this even more pronounced in government projects than in the private sector. Hence, in government projects, the project management team may also need to negotiate with representatives of civil service employees.

.3 Acquisition

See Section 9.2.2.3 of the *PMBOK® Guide*—Third Edition.

.4 Virtual Teams

See Section 9.2.2.4 of the *PMBOK® Guide*—Third Edition.

.5 Hybrid Staff

Government agencies occasionally contract for temporary human resources, whereby the government pays the actual salary and overhead for such employees. Such an arrangement allows the agency to rapidly "staff up and down" to meet project human resource requirements. Another rationale for use of such arrangements occurs in jurisdictions that are legally prohibited from recognizing employee organizations (e.g., labor unions). Such temporary human resources are not civil service employees, and are often called contract employees. While there is a fee paid to the contractor firm, such contract employees are not themselves independent contractors. On many government projects, the project staff is comprised of both temporary contract employees and permanent government employees—and this kind of combination is known as *hybrid staff*. Contract employees are typically integrated into a project staff for the duration of a project. A project manager often supervises such contract employees much like other staff—except for certain personnel matters (e.g., benefits and compensation) (see also Section 9.3.1 of the *PMBOK® Guide*—Third Edition).

.6 Prevailing Wages

See Section 12.5.2.9 of this *Government Extension*.

9.2.3 Acquire Project Team: Outputs

See Section 9.2.3 of the *PMBOK® Guide*—Third Edition.

9.3 Develop Project Team

See Section 9.3 of the *PMBOK® Guide*—Third Edition.

9.4 Manage Project Team

See Section 9.4 of the *PMBOK® Guide*—Third Edition.

Chapter 10

Project Communications Management

See the introduction to Chapter 10 in the *PMBOK® Guide* —Third Edition.

10.1 Communications Planning

See Section 10.1 of the *PMBOK® Guide*—Third Edition.

10.1.1 Communications Planning: Inputs

.1 Enterprise Environmental Factors

All the factors described in Section 4.1.1.3 are used as inputs for this process. However, as most government projects require some sort of public communication, the social and political factors listed in Section 4.1.1.3 have a significant impact on planning the communication scope, channels, and timing.

.2 Organizational Process Assets

While all of the assets described in Section 4.1.1.4 are used as inputs for this process, project managers may be limited as to what they are permitted to keep confidential. Public records laws give citizens in many countries the right to view almost all governmental records, with a few exceptions for secrecy and privacy protection.

.3 Project Scope Statement

See Section 10.1.1.3 of the *PMBOK® Guide*—Third Edition.

.4 Project Management Plan

In addition to constraints and assumptions listed in Section 10.1.1.4 of the *PMBOK® Guide*—Third Edition, the following comments are specific to government activity:

- **Constraints.** A likely constraint in government projects is a lack of understanding about the complexity of the communication processes on the part of team

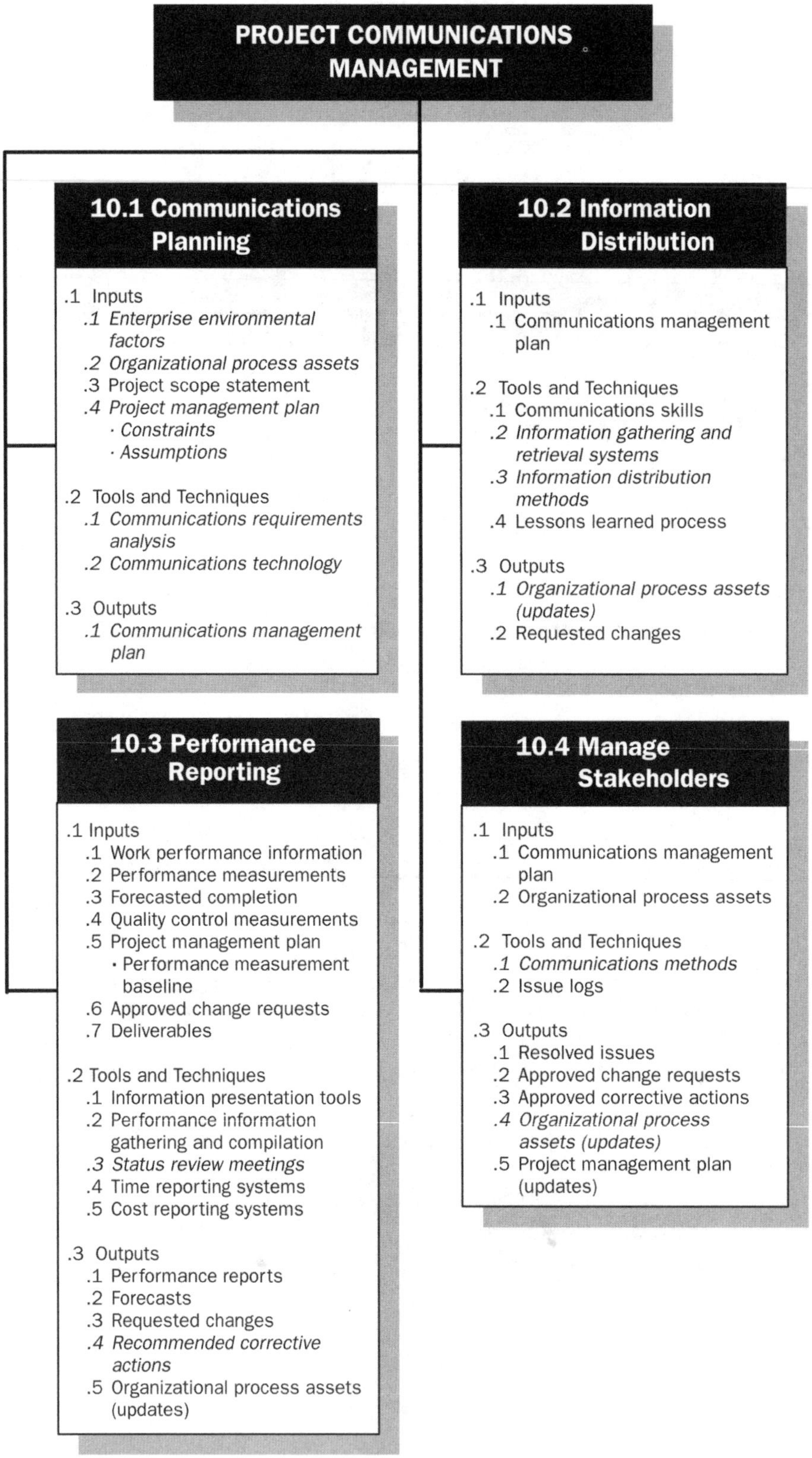

PROJECT COMMUNICATIONS MANAGEMENT

10.1 Communications Planning

.1 Inputs
   .1 *Enterprise environmental factors*
   .2 *Organizational process assets*
   .3 Project scope statement
   .4 *Project management plan*
     · Constraints
     · Assumptions

.2 Tools and Techniques
   .1 *Communications requirements analysis*
   .2 *Communications technology*

.3 Outputs
   .1 *Communications management plan*

10.2 Information Distribution

.1 Inputs
   .1 Communications management plan

.2 Tools and Techniques
   .1 Communications skills
   .2 *Information gathering and retrieval systems*
   .3 *Information distribution methods*
   .4 Lessons learned process

.3 Outputs
   .1 *Organizational process assets (updates)*
   .2 Requested changes

10.3 Performance Reporting

.1 Inputs
   .1 Work performance information
   .2 Performance measurements
   .3 Forecasted completion
   .4 Quality control measurements
   .5 Project management plan
     · Performance measurement baseline
   .6 Approved change requests
   .7 Deliverables

.2 Tools and Techniques
   .1 Information presentation tools
   .2 Performance information gathering and compilation
   .3 *Status review meetings*
   .4 Time reporting systems
   .5 Cost reporting systems

.3 Outputs
   .1 Performance reports
   .2 Forecasts
   .3 Requested changes
   .4 *Recommended corrective actions*
   .5 Organizational process assets (updates)

10.4 Manage Stakeholders

.1 Inputs
   .1 Communications management plan
   .2 Organizational process assets

.2 Tools and Techniques
   .1 *Communications methods*
   .2 Issue logs

.3 Outputs
   .1 Resolved issues
   .2 Approved change requests
   .3 Approved corrective actions
   .4 *Organizational process assets (updates)*
   .5 Project management plan (updates)

Figure 10-1. Project Communications Management

members, sponsors, and other stakeholders. In many government projects, contracted vendors/consultants (sellers) run the project day-to-day, reporting to an appointed government employee (project manager) who may have a limited project management background (or be selected as project manager based on technical expertise, rather than project management skills). The project documents (especially external communication) might also be constrained by multiple reporting formats, which are sometimes not compatible, and are required in internationally funded projects by donors (e.g., World Bank, IMF, etc.) or aid-giving countries. The project documents (especially external communication) might also be more formal and require the appropriate signatures.

- **Assumptions.** The primary assumption is that the project team will be working with or for a governing body, its officials (in the case of a representative government), and its constituents.

10.1.2 Communications Planning: Tools and Techniques

.1 Communications Requirements Analysis

Beyond the considerations expressed in Section 10.1.2.1 of the *PMBOK® Guide*—Third Edition, the information needs of organizational stakeholders have unique requirements based on information sharing in a functional bureaucracy. Government departments tend to be compartmentalized, so special planning is required when multiple departments, branches, agencies, or ministries are involved in the same project.

Project stakeholders include not only the office holders, but also the public (that is, the constituents, those governed, the taxpayers). Therefore, timely and appropriate information needs to be clearly understood by a broader range of affected individuals than is the case for most private sector projects.

Analysis and planning to manage the information and consultation needs for all stakeholders can be beneficial in obtaining balanced outcomes. For publicly funded projects, accountability to the public and the openness of political debate need to be factored in during project planning.

.2 Communications Technology

The compatibility of technologies used to transfer information can vary significantly from one agency or sphere of government to another. The availability of funding for technology upgrades to mitigate communications inconsistencies should be factored into the communications planning.

With wide (and ever-growing) public acceptance of the Internet, a government's relationship with its citizens relies more and more on specific tools for Web-based communication, such as official Web sites and government portals. E-government initiatives are currently undertaken by many national, regional, and local government bodies as an efficient way to provide information and services to the general public.

10.1.3 Communications Planning: Outputs

Section 10.1.3 of the *PMBOK® Guide*—Third Edition discusses the communications management plan as one output from Communications Planning. This is also produced on government projects, and has a particular application in government:

.1 Communications Management Plan

On government projects, government officials (rather than the project manager) sometimes possess control over the communications. This can work well, but when it does not, it can become difficult to pinpoint reasons for the communication breakdown.

10.2 Information Distribution

See Section 10.2 of the *PMBOK® Guide*—Third Edition.

10.2.1 Information Distribution: Inputs

See Section 10.2.1 of the *PMBOK® Guide*—Third Edition.

10.2.2 Information Distribution: Tools and Techniques

See Section 10.2.2 of the *PMBOK® Guide*—Third Edition, with the following additional comments:

.2 Information Gathering and Retrieval Systems

Specific laws adopted in many countries require government systems to apply a more rigorous security policy to maintain higher levels of data and communications security, and to preserve citizens' privacy, while still safeguarding the freedom of information rights related to accessing governmental records.

.3 Information Distribution Methods

In addition to the information distribution methods listed in Section 10.2.2.3 of the *PMBOK® Guide*—Third Edition, government projects often require public information dissemination through mass media communications, press conferences, public reports, investigations, audit results, and so on.

10.2.3 Information Distribution: Outputs

See Section 10.2.3 of the *PMBOK® Guide*—Third Edition, with the following additional comment:

.1 Organizational Process Assets (Updates)

Because the ultimate stakeholders in all government projects are citizens, the "stakeholder notifications" component in Section 10.2.3.1 of the *PMBOK® Guide*—Third Edition must also include public information communication.

Also, government audit or public accounts committees often require project information (all project records, not only the final reports) to be archived for a minimum period of time, such as 5–10 years after completion of the project. Project records may include correspondence, memos, reports (written or electronic), audio or video recordings, presentations of content, and any other document describing and detailing the project. This information may become available to the public, or be made available via freedom of information requests or similar processes, depending on the government sponsoring the project.

10.3 Performance Reporting

See Section 10.3 of the *PMBOK® Guide*—Third Edition.

10.3.1 Performance Reporting: Inputs

Section 10.3.1 of the *PMBOK® Guide*—Third Edition discusses inputs to Performance Reporting. All of these are used on government projects, but their formats may be prescribed by government components (such as defense or transportation), or have matching formats across all agencies. Also, election cycles can influence the reporting timelines required by representative bodies and executives.

If a project is outsourced, vendors or consultants will likely submit project reports to the government employee project manager responsible for the work.

10.3.2 Performance Reporting: Tools and Techniques

See Section 10.3.2 of the *PMBOK® Guide*—Third Edition, with the addition of the following:

.3 **Status Review Meetings**
For public sector projects, status review meetings usually include periodic reviews by funding or supervising authorities, such as a management review board year-end review, planning and development department's quarterly review of projects, World Bank review missions, etc.

10.3.3 Performance Reporting: Outputs

See Section 10.3.3 of the *PMBOK® Guide*—Third Edition, with the addition of the following:

.4 **Recommended Corrective Actions**
Frequently, requested changes include budget adjustments as an important output of performance review. In the government context, projects are assigned annual budgets. If the funds cannot be utilized during the annual period, they are often returned unspent to the funding source. Additional funds may have to be requested to align the planned scope with the project baseline (see Section 7.2 of this document).

10.4 Manage Stakeholders

See Section 10.4 of the *PMBOK® Guide*—Third Edition.

10.4.1 Manage Stakeholders: Inputs

See Section 10.4.1 of the *PMBOK® Guide*—Third Edition.

10.4.2 Manage Stakeholders: Tools and Techniques

See Section 10.4.2 of the *PMBOK® Guide*—Third Edition, with the addition of the following:

.1 Communications Methods

Beyond the communications methods listed in Section 10.4.2.1 of the *PMBOK® Guide*—Third Edition, those in a government environment include specific tools for information distribution to parliamentary organizations and the general public. Such tools include government reports, presentations to legislative bodies, mass media communications, news conferences, public notices, and Web postings (among others), and are important to managing relationships with these key stakeholders.

10.4.3 Manage Stakeholders: Outputs

See Section 10.4.3 of the *PMBOK® Guide*—Third Edition, with the addition of the following:

.4 Organizational Process Assets (Updates)

For public sector projects, updates to organizational process assets also include external communication to public and other official organizations that contribute to a general government perception.

Chapter 11

Project Risk Management

According to the *PMBOK® Guide*—Third Edition, "Project Risk Management includes the processes concerned with conducting risk management planning, identification, analysis, responses, and monitoring and control on a project; most of these processes are updated throughout the project. The objectives of Project Risk Management are to increase the probability and impact of positive events, and decrease the probability and impact of events adverse to the project."

The *PMBOK® Guide*—Third Edition describes six processes in the Project Risk Management Knowledge Area:

11.1 Risk Management Planning
11.2 Risk Identification
11.3 Qualitative Risk Analysis
11.4 Quantitative Risk Analysis
11.5 Risk Response Planning
11.6 Risk Monitoring and Control

Government projects follow the same processes, but the project risks include social, environmental, and political risks, in addition to financial risks. Many government projects would be rejected or abandoned if they were subjected to objective financial analysis, as typically used in the private sector. For example, a return on investment (ROI) analysis considers both upside risk (e.g., profit potential) and downside risk (e.g., loss potential). Government projects often do not demonstrate a profit potential, but are intended to generate a return through benefits to the public-at-large or to a segment of the public. A well-known example is the International Space Station Program. This program posed immense risk of financial and human loss, and had virtually no potential for profit. Although it is considered a huge success by all governments involved, such programs would have been completely unacceptable in the private sector unless the upside benefits outweighed the downside risks. In contrast to objective financial analysis in the private sector, the success of a government project may also be evaluated according to subjective criteria, such as values held by stakeholders—the citizens—through their government body.

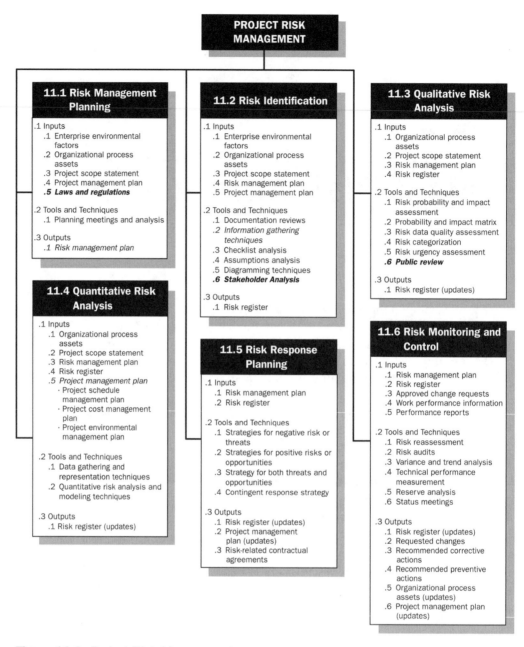

Figure 11-1. Project Risk Management

11.1 Risk Management Planning

See Section 11.1 of the *PMBOK® Guide*—Third Edition.

11.1.1 Risk Management Planning: Inputs

Section 11.1.1 of the *PMBOK® Guide*—Third Edition discusses four inputs to Risk Management Planning. An additional input has application in government projects:

.5 Laws and Regulations

Citizens, through their government body, establish mandatory practices for government projects in the form of laws and regulations. These laws and regulations establish limitations on each project and define risks that the citizens will not accept. Hence, these laws and regulations are intended to manage risk, although such laws generally do not use the word "risk." Laws and regulations, as expressed in mandatory policies and practices, become incorporated into organizational process assets (such as those described in Section 11.1.1.2 of the *PMBOK® Guide*—Third Edition). Some of these policies and practices may relate to:

- Air and water quality
- Affirmative action and assistance to disadvantaged groups
- Archeological, historical, and architectural preservation
- Mitigation of impacts to affected businesses and communities
- Endangered species protection
- Protection of endangered ecological systems such as wetlands, grasslands, or waterways
- Noise or sound mitigation
- Religious freedom and the protection of sacred places
- Protection of scenic areas and parks.

Several of the above categories are often combined into an omnibus environmental protection law.

11.1.2 Risk Management Planning: Tools and Techniques

See Section 11.1.2 of the *PMBOK® Guide*—Third Edition.

11.1.3 Risk Management Planning: Outputs

See Section 11.1.3.1 of the *PMBOK® Guide*—Third Edition. In addition to the outputs described in this section, the following additional information pertaining to risk categories is relevant to public sector projects:

- **Risk Categories.** In government projects, political risk is another subcategory within the external risk category. Government projects are more susceptible to political risk than projects in the private sector. Each phase of a government project is typically subject to government approval. In addition, government priorities can change for various reasons, reflecting a change in the will of the citizens as expressed through the election process. Thus, if government priorities change before approval of the final phase of a project, the project could be halted prior to completion—a significant political risk (see Figure 11-4).

Sources of political risk vary and may include, for example:

- **Various Levels of Government Organizations.** Stakeholders in a nation or region—and their national or regional government body—may support a project, while local stakeholders—and their local government body—may oppose the project. This is often associated with the NIMBY ("not in my back yard") syndrome. From a national or regional perspective, stakeholders may support a project (e.g., a hazardous waste disposal facility), but local stakeholders may oppose it.
- **Other stakeholder conflicts.** For instance, stakeholders may want to commute to work alone each day in their private automobiles, but other stakeholders support reducing air pollution by promoting the use of high-occupancy vehicles or carpooling. In some cases, stakeholders may not be sure about their priorities.
- **Changes over time.** Stakeholders may support a project when funds are plentiful, but may later oppose the project when funds are scarce and tax increases are needed to complete it.

11.2 Risk Identification

See Section 11.2 of the *PMBOK® Guide*—Third Edition.

11.2.1 Risk Identification: Inputs

See Section 11.2.1 of the *PMBOK® Guide*—Third Edition.

11.2.2 Risk Identification: Tools and Techniques

Section 11.2.2 of the *PMBOK® Guide*—Third Edition discusses tools and techniques for Risk Identification. In two of these areas, Information Gathering Techniques and Stakeholder Analysis, additional tools and techniques are relevant to government projects:

.2 **Information Gathering Techniques**

Section 11.2.2.2 of the *PMBOK® Guide*—Third Edition discusses the following techniques for information gathering: brainstorming; Delphi technique; interviewing; root cause identification; and strengths, weaknesses, opportunities, and threats (SWOT) analysis. These techniques are generally the same for government projects, but the focus can be different. On government projects, these techniques focus on factors of concern to the citizens and their government body. In government projects, for instance, risks associated with cost and schedule may be far less important than those associated with other factors, such as environmental protection and affirmative action.

In addition to the techniques described in Section 11.2.2.2 of the *PMBOK® Guide*—Third Edition, field research and surveys can be especially valuable on government projects:

- **Field research.** Field research is essential in environmental areas such as air and water quality, the protection of endangered species, and noise mitigation. Specialists need to perform field observations and tests to ascertain how a project might affect these factors.
- **Interviewing.** Interviewing is useful in identifying some citizens' social concerns such as affirmative action; archeological, historical, and architectural preservation; and the protection of scenic areas. In government projects, interviewing is also called "surveys."

.6 **Stakeholder Analysis**

Section 11.2.2.2 discusses the use of interviewing as an information gathering technique. After interviewing stakeholders, analysis can be performed on information gathered from the stakeholders.

11.2.3 Risk Identification: Outputs

See Section 11.2.3 of the *PMBOK® Guide*—Third Edition.

11.3 Qualitative Risk Analysis

See Section 11.3 of the *PMBOK® Guide*—Third Edition.

11.3.1 Qualitative Risk Analysis: Inputs

See Section 11.3.1 of the *PMBOK® Guide*—Third Edition.

11.3.2 Qualitative Risk Analysis: Tools and Techniques

Section 11.3.2 of the *PMBOK® Guide*—Third Edition discusses tools and techniques for Qualitative Risk Analysis. One additional tool has application on government projects:

.6 **Public Review**

If there is any controversial issue relating to a government project, the project is often subjected to scrutiny through public review. This allows a government body to gauge the will of its citizens. Public review can include public meetings and/or publication of documents for review and comment. Public meetings can have varied formats, including formal hearings before a government body; formal presentations to a public audience followed by a question and answer session; and public workshops. Public requests for review and comment are often required before or after a public meeting, especially in regard to environmental documentation. Some of the best practices in public review include:

- **Holding public debates between supporters and opponents of a project.** Every project has advantages and disadvantages. Supporters and opponents of the project need an opportunity to present their arguments for or against a project in a clear, logical manner. Often, supporters of the project have more resources and information and, thus, are better prepared to present their arguments. Unfortunately, this can leave opponents to respond mainly on an emotional level. Emotions do not inform the public or contribute to a search for the best alternative. Hence, public review may involve helping opponents of the project present their arguments. Project resources must, therefore, be committed to helping opponents articulate their case and place all feasible alternative choices before the public and the representative body.
- **Holding workshops rather than public hearings or formal presentations.** In a public workshop, different aspects of the project are described at booths or information stations. At several stations, there are recording devices for people to give their opinions. Members of the public move from booth to booth to learn about the project and present opinions. In this way, everyone has the opportunity to participate. In public hearings, by contrast, there is one public place where people can address the assembly. Participation in hearings is limited to those who feel strongly about the project or who enjoy public speaking. Most people do not participate. Workshops are more interactive, give a better gauge of public opinion, and are more useful in developing logical arguments and alternatives.

11.3.3 Qualitative Risk Analysis: Outputs

See Section 11.3.3 of the *PMBOK® Guide*—Third Edition.

11.4 Quantitative Risk Analysis

See Section 11.4 of the *PMBOK® Guide*—Third Edition.

Quantitative Risk Analysis on government projects utilizes characteristics similar to those of private sector projects. However, unlike private sector projects, government project risk is not expressed only in terms of cost and schedule. Risks relating to social and environmental concerns may have much greater weight than risks relating to a project's cost and schedule, as well as those relating to scope.

11.4.1 Quantitative Risk Analysis: Inputs

Section 11.4.1 of the *PMBOK® Guide*—Third Edition discusses inputs to Quantitative Risk Analysis. An additional input, under "project management plan," has application on government projects:

> .5 **Project Management Plan**
> See Section 11.4.1.5 of the *PMBOK® Guide*—Third Edition.
> - **Project environmental management plan.** On government projects, a risk management plan often includes environmental management planning. For example, a risk management plan may include a storm water runoff management plan. In addition, a risk management plan may include mitigation plans for other environmental concerns, such as impacts to neighboring businesses and communities.

11.4.2 Quantitative Risk Analysis: Tools and Techniques

See Section 11.4.2 of the *PMBOK® Guide*—Third Edition.

11.4.3 Quantitative Risk Analysis: Outputs

See Section 11.4.3 of the *PMBOK® Guide*—Third Edition.

11.5 Risk Response Planning

See Section 11.5 of the *PMBOK® Guide*—Third Edition.

11.6 Risk Monitoring and Control

See Section 11.6 of the *PMBOK® Guide*—Third Edition.

Chapter 12

Project Procurement Management

According to the *PMBOK® Guide*—Third Edition, "Project Procurement Management includes the processes to purchase or acquire the products, services, or results needed from outside the project team to perform the work," as well as the contract management and change control processes to administer any contract issued by authorized project team members, by the performing organization (normally the seller), or the outside organization (normally the buyer).

In government projects, the performing organization can be the responsible government agency, because its employees are often the most directly involved in doing the work of the project. However, for certain projects known as "turnkey" projects (e.g., design-build-operate-transfer), the seller would be the performing organization—and the government the outside organization—because the seller is the enterprise whose employees are most directly involved in doing the work of the project (see Section 12.2).

Governments around the world invest enormous amounts of money in project procurement. In the United States alone, government procurement in the construction industry amounted to $230 billion in 2004. To estimate the total government project procurement, one must also add government procurement in other countries and expand to other industries, such as health and human services, aerospace, defense, environmental, financial, oil, gas, petroleum, utilities, and communications technologies.

This enormous magnitude of government procurement presents significant challenges in achieving efficiency, integrity, and equity in government procurement. Meeting these challenges is essential to achieving the efficient use of government resources, to maintain the public trust, and to ensure open and fair competition among prospective government contractors (hereafter referred to as "sellers"). To be effective, Project Procurement Management must be institutionalized within the organization. A first step is to have government procurement decisions made by government officials who are accountable to the public through procurement regulations, protest procedures, conflict of interest laws, and other similar provisions. Another step is to encourage sellers to recognize the integral roles of their organizations in meeting these challenges.

Hence, Project Procurement Management should serve the following purposes:

- Provide an open, fair, and competitive process that minimizes opportunities for corruption and that assures the impartial selection of a seller

- Avoid potential and actual conflicts of interest, or the appearance of a conflict of interest
- Establish an objective basis for seller selection
- Obtain the best value in terms of price and quality
- Document the requirements that a seller must meet in order to obtain payment
- Provide a basis for evaluating and overseeing the work of the seller
- Allow flexible arrangements for obtaining products and services given the particular circumstances, provided such arrangements do not violate the other purposes of Project Procurement Management.

The *PMBOK® Guide*—Third Edition describes six processes under the Project Procurement Management Knowledge Area:

12.1 **Plan Purchases and Acquisitions**
12.2 **Plan Contracting**
12.3 **Request Seller Responses**
12.4 **Select Sellers**
12.5 **Contract Administration**
12.6 **Contract Closure**

12.1 Plan Purchases and Acquisitions

See Section 12.1 of the *PMBOK® Guide*—Third Edition.

12.1.1 Plan Purchases and Acquisitions: Inputs

Section 12.1.1 of the *PMBOK® Guide*—Third Edition discusses inputs to Plan Purchases and Acquisitions. Although all of these inputs apply in government procurement of projects, the first two of these categories should also include additional inputs that apply especially to procurement in public sector projects:

.1 **Enterprise Environmental Factors**

Enterprise environmental factors (Section 4.1.1.3) that are considered in most projects include the conditions of the marketplace and what products, services, and results are available in the marketplace, from whom, and under what terms and conditions. On government projects, certain marketplace conditions may differ from those in the private sector. For example, some sellers target specific market sectors (e.g., consumer, commercial, etc.) and position themselves to meet the needs of those sectors. As a result, there may be fewer sellers that are both capable and willing to contract with the government.

If the performing organization does not have formal purchasing and contracting groups, then the project team will have to supply both the resources and the expertise to perform project procurement activities. On government projects, the government generally acts as the performing organization, and has formal purchasing and contracting groups that perform procurement activities, including the awarding of contracts to outside organizations.

.2 **Organizational Process Assets**

Organizational process assets (Section 4.1.1.4) provide the formal and informal procurement-related policies, procedures, guidelines, and management systems that are considered in developing the procurement management plan and selecting the contract types to be used. Organizational policies frequently constrain

PROJECT PROCUREMENT MANAGEMENT

12.1 Plan Purchases and Acquisitions

.1 Inputs
  .1 *Enterprise environmental factors*
  .2 *Organizational process assets*
  .3 Project scope statement
  .4 Work breakdown structure
  .5 WBS dictionary
  .6 Project management plan
    · Risk register
    · Risk-related contractual agreements
    · Resource requirements
    · Project schedule
    · Activity cost estimate
    · Cost baseline

.2 Tools and Techniques
  .1 Make-or-buy analysis
  .2 Expert judgment
  .3 *Contract types*
  .4 Degrees of competition
  .5 Degrees of qualification

.3 Outputs
  .1 *Procurement management plan*
  .2 Contract statement of work
  .3 Make-or-buy decisions
  .4 Requested changes

12.4 Select Sellers

.1 Inputs
  .1 Organizational process assets
  .2 Procurement management plan
  .3 Evaluation criteria
  .4 Procurement document package
  .5 Proposals
  .6 Qualified sellers list
  .7 Project management plan
    · Risk register
    · Risk-related contractual agreements

.2 Tools and Techniques
  .1 *Weighting system*
  .2 Independent estimates
  .3 Screening system
  .4 Contract negotiation
  .5 Seller rating systems
  .6 Expert judgment
  .7 *Proposal evaluation techniques*
  .8 Award and preference laws
  .9 Protest and grievance procedures

.3 Outputs
  .1 Selected sellers
  .2 Contract
  .3 Contract management plan
  .4 Resource availability

12.2 Plan Contracting

.1 Inputs
  .1 Procurement management plan
  .2 Contract statement of work
  .3 Make-or-buy decisions
  .4 Project management plan
    · Risk register
    · Risk-related contractual agreements
    · Resource requirements
    · Project schedule
    · Activity cost estimate
    · Cost baseline

.2 Tools and Techniques
  .1 *Standard forms*
  .2 Expert judgment

.3 Outputs
  .1 Procurement documents
  .2 Evaluation criteria
  .3 Contract statement of work (updates)

12.5 Contract Administration

.1 Inputs
  .1 Contract
  .2 Contract management plan
  .3 Selected sellers
  .4 Performance reports
  .5 Approved change requests
  .6 *Work performance information*
  .7 Claims

.2 Tools and Techniques
  .1 Contract change control system
  .2 Buyer-conducted performance review
  .3 *Inspections and audits*
  .4 Performance reporting
  .5 Payment system
  .6 *Claims administration*
  .7 Records management system
  .8 Information technology
  .9 Prevailing wages

.3 Outputs
  .1 Contract documentation
  .2 Requested changes
  .3 Recommended corrective actions
  .4 Organizational process assets (updates)
  .5 Project management plan (updates)
    · Procurement management plan
    · Contract management

12.3 Request Seller Responses

.1 Inputs
  .1 Organizational process assets
  .2 Procurement management plan
  .3 Procurement documents

.2 Tools and Techniques
  .1 *Bidder conferences*
  .2 *Advertising*
  .3 *Develop qualified sellers list*

.3 Outputs
  .1 *Qualified sellers list*
  .2 Procurement document package
  .3 Proposals

12.6 Contract Closure

.1 Inputs
  .1 Procurement management plan
  .2 Contract management plan
  .3 Contract documentation
  .4 Contract closure procedure

.2 Tools and Techniques
  .1 *Procurement audits*
  .2 Records management system

.3 Outputs
  .1 Closed contracts
  .2 *Organizational process assets (updates)*

Figure 12-1. Project Procurement Management

procurement decisions. These policy constraints can include limiting the use of purchase orders and requiring all purchases above a certain amount to use a longer form of contract, requiring specific forms of contracts, limiting the ability to make specific make-or-buy decisions, and limiting or requiring specific types or sizes of sellers.

In government procurement, most constraints are formal rules established by the controlling representative body. These constraints can also include requiring advertising of contract opportunities prior to their award, sealed bids or proposals from sellers, and open public bids or proposals. These constraints are typically comprised of the following:

- **An open, fair, and competitive process for selecting and awarding contracted services.** An open, fair, and competitive process is designed to ensure that the project obtains the best value, to prevent collusion and corruption, and to afford an opportunity to all responsible sellers.
- **The evaluation method and basis of award published in advance.** Publishing the method to be used to evaluate sellers and the basis of award to the selected seller establishes a level playing field.
- **The level of funding authorized by the representative body.** The funding authorized by the representative body may not be exceeded without an additional appropriation by the representative body.
- **Programs to achieve social and economic goals.** These programs can include preferences for disadvantaged population groups and preferences for small businesses.

Organizations in some application areas also have an established multi-tier supplier system of selected and pre-qualified sellers to reduce the number of direct sellers to the organization and establish an extended supply system. In government procurement, establishing a supplier system can include competitive selection of a seller as the primary supplier for a certain category of products or services. However, if the value of the project is above a certain amount, the seller may still be required to compete with other potential sellers. In each of these competitions, utilization of a pre-qualification procedure is intended to attract better qualified sellers.

12.1.2 Plan Purchases and Acquisitions: Tools and Techniques

Section 12.1.2 of the *PMBOK® Guide*—Third Edition discusses three tools and techniques for Plan Purchases and Acquisitions. In the third of these, Contract Types, several additional tools have particular application on government projects. Two other categories of government project-specific tools and techniques are also added: Degrees of Competition and Degrees of Qualification:

.3 Contract Types

See Section 12.1.2.3 of the *PMBOK® Guide*—Third Edition, which discusses three broad categories of contract types. There are other important contract types used in government projects, as discussed below:

- **Indefinite delivery indefinite quantity contracts (IDIQ).** Some agencies also call these "job-order," "on call," or "standby" contracts. The contract typically states the type of service to be delivered, the length of time (generally five years or less) during which services can be requested from the seller, and the minimum and maximum of the contract amount. Additionally, the contract typically includes a "price book." Each potential seller submits a markup or markdown in the form of a coefficient (e.g., 1.1 or 0.9). Many agencies utilize this method of obtaining services for small projects. Seller selection is a time-consuming process. To go through this process for each project is often inefficient and may cause unacceptable delays. IDIQ increases efficiency and minimizes delay by performing the selection process once for many projects. In many cases, the IDIQ contract is in place before the start of a project. With the contract in place, a project manager for the government can obtain the necessary services without having to go through a separate solicitation process. This streamlined process supports small, non-complex projects.

- **Unit price contract.** Unit price contracts are a special category of fixed price contract. Unit prices are ideally based on standard units of measurement (e.g., man-hour, linear foot, cubic meter). A unit price contract typically states estimated quantities and fixed prices for each unit of work. Many agencies use this type of contract for projects where the actual quantities of work may vary from the estimated quantities.

- **Multiple award schedules.** Multiple award schedules can be used when there is a generally accepted "reasonable price" for a good or service. Multiple award schedules are particularly valuable for procurement of commodities. Each potential seller submits its qualifications and schedule of rates to the government procurement office. Assuming each schedule of rates is based on generally accepted "reasonable" prices. The government procurement office can select the seller that is most advantageous to the government. If these are approved, government agencies may buy goods and services at the published rates without a separate competition. In many jurisdictions, this type of contract is fairly new and often requires specific legislation because of the long-term nature of the relationship. This method is often adopted as a strategic sourcing initiative and supported by W. Edwards Deming's fourth point for management, "End the practice of awarding business on the basis of price tag. Instead, minimize total cost. Move toward a single supplier for any one item, on a long-term relationship of loyalty and trust."

.4 Degrees of Competition

- **Full and open competition.** All responsible sources are allowed to compete. This is the most commonly used contracting approach in government procurement.

- **Other than full and open competition.** Some government agencies exclude one or more sellers from competing. Depending on the scenario, the degree of competition can range from a group of sellers to a single seller. Common scenarios are discussed below:

  (a) *Set-aside.* A set-aside for small businesses or disadvantaged firms is an example of this method. Alternatively, a government agency may establish minimum targets or "goals" for participation by small businesses and disadvantaged firms, which the seller must demonstrate good faith efforts to achieve. Another example is that some procurement opportunities are open to international sellers; others are restricted to national companies.

  (b) *Sole-source.* A "sole-source" contract is used where permissible by law when there is only a single seller that can perform the work—by reason of experience, possession of specialized facilities, or technical competence—in a time frame required by the government. This type of contract requires a written justification to be approved by an authorized government official.

(c) Eminent domain. Eminent domain has been in use for thousands of years, and is probably the oldest form of government procurement under established legal systems (e.g., Roman law, the Magna Carta, the Code Napoleon, and the Constitution of the United States. The government may take possession of private property when this action is in the best interest of the public. Eminent domain is used most often to take possession of real property. The government is generally required to pay just (i.e., fair) compensation for the property.

.5 Degrees of Qualification

All government contracts require that the seller meet minimum qualifications listed in the procurement documents. Assuming these minimum qualifications are met, the degree of qualification depends on the basis of selection. There are some common approaches:

- **Lowest responsible seller.** This approach is the most common basis for selection in government procurement. Potential sellers' bids or proposals are evaluated to ensure that they meet minimum qualifications. Then, the cost proposals of the qualified sellers are reviewed and the lowest responsible seller is selected. For example, in a construction contract, the minimum qualifications are generally a contractor's license, liability insurance, and a payment and performance bond. However, the minimum qualifications may vary. For example, minimum qualifications may also include financial solvency, a satisfactory safety record, and successful performance on comparable projects.
- **Best value based on price and qualifications.** Sellers' bids or proposals are evaluated to ensure that they meet minimum qualifications. Then, the technical and cost proposals of the qualified sellers are reviewed. Sellers are evaluated by a combination of several factors including price and qualifications, with a predetermined weight assigned to each factor. A weight may be assigned to the price as part of the weighted sum, or the unweighted price may be divided by the weighted sum of other factors to determine the cost per point. The contract is then awarded to the seller that has the highest weighted score or lowest cost per point, whichever is applicable. This is also known as a best value selection.
- **Qualifications-based selection.** This basis of selection is most often used on contracts for professional services. Price is generally not a factor in selection of professional services during project planning and design because the cost of such services is a small fraction of the project's implementation cost. For example, increased quality in the planning and design of a building can result in large savings via the cost of construction of the building. Sellers' qualifications are evaluated, the sellers are ranked, and a contract is negotiated with the best qualified firm. If the government and the seller are unable to agree on a reasonable price, the government terminates the negotiations and begins negotiating with the second-ranked firm, etc.

12.1.3 Plan Purchases and Acquisitions: Outputs

.1 Procurement Management Plan

Section 12.1.3.1 of the *PMBOK® Guide—Third Edition* says "The procurement management plan describes how the procurement processes will be managed from developing procurement documentation through contract closure." In government procurement, a major driver is the applicable set of procurement laws, rules, and regulations. Hence, the procurement management plan should reference the requirements of any applicable laws, rules and regulations. The *PMBOK® Guide*—Third Edition lists the following elements of a procurement management plan, to which has been added another element: "Constraints and Assumptions":

- Types of contracts to be used
- Who will prepare independent estimates and if they are needed as evaluation criteria
- Those actions the project management team can take on its own, if the performing organization has a procurement, contracting, or purchasing department
- Standardized procurement documents, if they are needed
- Managing multiple providers
- Coordinating procurement with other project aspects, such as scheduling and performance reporting
- Handling the lead times required to purchase or acquire items from sellers and coordinating them with the project schedule development
- Handling the make-or-buy decisions and linking them into the Activity Resource Estimating and Schedule Development processes
- Setting the scheduled dates in each contract for the contract deliverables and coordinating with the schedule development and control processes
- Identifying performance bonds or insurance contracts to mitigate some forms of project risk
- Establishing the form and format to be used for the contract statement of work
- Identifying pre-qualified selected sellers, if any, to be used
- Procurement metrics to be used to manage contracts and evaluate sellers.
- Constraints and assumptions that could affect planned purchases and acquisitions. Examples of constraints include: Whether and to what extent advertising of the contracting opportunity is required and the selection process to be used including the basis of award.

A procurement management plan can be formal or informal, can be detailed or broadly framed, and is based upon the needs of the project. The procurement management plan is a subsidiary component of the project management plan (Section 4.3).

.2 Contract Statement of Work
See Section 12.1.3.2 of the *PMBOK® Guide*—Third Edition.

.3 Make-or-Buy Decisions
See Section 12.1.3.3 of the *PMBOK® Guide*—Third Edition.

.4 Requested Changes
See Section 12.1.3.4 of the *PMBOK® Guide*—Third Edition.

12.2 Plan Contracting
See Section 12.2 of the *PMBOK® Guide*—Third Edition.

12.2.1 Plan Contracting: Inputs

See Section 12.2.1 of the *PMBOK® Guide*—Third Edition.

12.2.2 Plan Contracting: Tools and Techniques

.1 Standard Forms

Standard forms include standard contracts, standard descriptions of procurement items, non-disclosure agreements, proposal evaluation criteria checklists, and standardized versions of all parts of the needed bid documents. Organizations that perform substantial amounts of procurement can have these documents standardized. Buyer and seller organizations performing intellectual property transactions should ensure that non-disclosures are approved and accepted before sharing any project-specific intellectual property with the other party.

In government procurement, the government often acts as the buyer and utilizes standard forms for bid documents (e.g., bid or proposal forms, bid bonds, payment and performance bonds) as well as other contract documents (e.g., general conditions, certificates of insurance, specifications) to ensure that the bid from each seller is based on the same terms and conditions.

.2 Expert Judgment

See Section 12.2.2.2 of the *PMBOK® Guide*—Third Edition.

12.2.3 Plan Contracting: Outputs

See Section 12.2.3 of the *PMBOK® Guide*—Third Edition.

12.3 Request Seller Responses

The Request Seller Responses process obtains responses, such as bids and proposals, from prospective sellers, normally at no cost to the project or buyer. In government procurement, there may be a relatively small cost to the project or buyer if a "stipend" is paid to one or more unsuccessful proposers to acquire rights to their technical proposals.

12.3.1 Request Seller Responses: Inputs

See Section 12.3.1 of the *PMBOK® Guide*—Third Edition.

12.3.2 Request Seller Responses: Tools and Techniques

Section 12.3.2 of the *PMBOK® Guide*—Third Edition discusses tools and techniques for Request Seller Responses. These have particular application in government procurement, and the following information should be considered, in addition to what is provided in the *PMBOK® Guide*—Third Edition:

.1 Bidder Conferences

In government procurement, bidder conferences are one of several types of permissible communications with potential sellers. Subject to prequalification by a government agency (see Section 12.3.2.3), all potential sellers are given equal standing during this initial buyer and seller interaction to produce the best bid, quote, or proposal. Communications between potential sellers and government officials are strictly controlled from the date a procurement document is issued until a seller is selected and a contract is awarded. The manner of communications is set forth in the procurement documents. Permissible communication consists of:

- **Meetings or conferences.** These meetings or conferences (also called contractor conferences, vendor conferences, and pre-bid conferences) are meetings with potential sellers *prior to* the preparation of a bid, quote, offer, or proposal. Such meetings are typically used to ensure that all potential sellers have a clear understanding of key information about the procurement (e.g., project, contract requirements, and the bidding process). A meeting or conference can be held in varied formats, such as face-to-face or via the Internet. A meeting or conference is often made a mandatory requirement to ensure that potential sellers make responsive bids. If a meeting or conference is held, the entire proceeding is normally scripted to ensure that key information is correctly understood by each of the potential sellers. If questions received during a meeting or conference are not covered by the prepared script, the questions and their corresponding answers are generally documented in writing.
- **Written procurement communications.** The government agency may issue communications, to respond to questions or inquiries from potential sellers, or to clarify procurement documents. Such communications are generally documented in writing, incorporated into the procurement documents, and distributed to all potential sellers who have provided an address for the receipt of such communications.
- **On-site inspection tours.** A site visit may be held by the government to provide the potential sellers with a clear understanding of the site issues relating to procurement. Any statements by the government agency are documented in the same way as other responses to questions from potential sellers.

.2 Advertising

Existing lists of potential sellers can often be expanded by placing advertisements in general circulation publications such as newspapers, or in specialty publications such as professional journals. Some government jurisdictions require public advertising of certain types of procurement initiatives, and most government jurisdictions require public advertising of pending government contracts. Such public advertising names the project and describes the contracting opportunity. For certain categories of projects (e.g., public works), the government requires advertisements to be published in general and/or trade publications circulated in the locality of the project. Many governments also publish a bulletin that lists all their contracts that are in the solicitation process. These include the *Commerce Business Daily* (United States government), *Government Gazette* (many governments), *California Contracts Register*, and similar publications.

.3 Develop Qualified Sellers List

Qualified sellers lists can be developed from the organizational assets if such lists or information are readily available. Whether or not that data is available, the project team can also develop its own sources. General information is widely available through the Internet, library directories, relevant local associations, trade catalogs, and similar sources. Detailed information on specific sources can require more extensive effort, such as site visits or contact with previous customers. Procurement documents (Section 12.2.3.1) can also be sent to determine if some or all of the prospective sellers have an interest in becoming a qualified potential seller.

In government procurement, there are several degrees of qualification (as described in Section 12.1.2.5 of this extension). To be considered a qualified seller by the government agency, a potential seller must have at least the minimum qualifications to perform the work of the project. This is also called seller responsibility. There are several methods of determining seller responsibility including prequalification of potential sellers. A government official may or may not elect to pre-qualify sellers. If the government elects to pre-qualify sellers, it may be required to advertise the contracting opportunity for contracts above a certain value and invite all responsible sellers to submit appropriate qualifications documents (e.g., pre-qualification questionnaire, statement of financial condition, statement of qualifications) in advance of a seller's proposal or quotation. A list of pre-qualified sellers can be developed for use on a specific project or developed on an annual basis for use on multiple projects. If a seller is pre-qualified for a specific project, the seller is not necessarily pre-qualified for general use.

12.3.3 Request Seller Responses: Outputs

Section 12.3.3 of *PMBOK® Guide*—Third Edition covers three outputs of the Request Seller Responses process. In the first of these, some additional information is relevant to government procurement:

.1 **Qualified Sellers List**
The qualified sellers list is comprised of those sellers who are asked to submit a proposal or quotation. In government procurement, the government is required to invite all qualified responsible sellers to submit a proposal or quotation for contracts above a certain value. Such an invitation normally takes the form of advertising (Section 12.3.2.2), but may also include additional outreach efforts. If the government pre-qualifies sellers, the qualified sellers list would consist of *only* the pre-qualified sellers (Section 12.3.2.3). However, if the government does not pre-qualify sellers, the qualified sellers list would comprise only potential sellers whose qualifications are yet to be determined until after receipt of their qualifications documents. Thus, governments may ask sellers to submit a proposal or quotation before determining whether those sellers are qualified.

.2 **Procurement Document Package**
See Section 12.3.3.2 of the *PMBOK® Guide*—Third Edition.

.3 **Proposals**
See Section 12.3.3.3 of the *PMBOK® Guide*—Third Edition.

12.4 Select Sellers

See Section 12.4 of the *PMBOK® Guide*—Third Edition.

12.4.1 Select Sellers: Inputs

See Section 12.4.1 of the *PMBOK® Guide*—Third Edition.

12.4.2 Select Sellers: Tools and Techniques

Section 12.4.2 of the *PMBOK® Guide*—Third Edition discusses seven tools and techniques for the Select Sellers process, which have varied application in government project procurement. Some comments—as well as two new tools—with special relevance to government projects have been added below:

.1 **Weighting System**

A weighting system is a method of quantifying qualitative data to minimize the effect of personal prejudice on seller selection. Most such systems involve assigning a numerical weight to each of the evaluation criteria, rating the prospective sellers on each criterion, multiplying the weight by the rating, and adding the resultant products to compute the overall score.

In government procurement, a weighting system is often set forth in the procurement documents, including the relative importance of each evaluation criterion.[1] When the basis of award is best value, the evaluation criteria includes price and other factors (e.g., experience, quality, financial condition) to determine the seller's proposal that is most advantageous to the government. If price is given a weight, the overall score is determined as described above. Alternatively, a technical score may be computed based on all criteria excluding price, after which price is divided by the technical score to determine the overall score. In this way, the highest ranked seller will be the seller having the lowest price per technical point, and debate on the relative importance of price can be avoided.

.2 **Independent Estimates**

See Section 12.4.2.2 of the *PMBOK® Guide*—Third Edition.

.3 **Screening System**

See Section 12.4.2.3 of the *PMBOK® Guide*—Third Edition.

.4 **Contract Negotiation**

In government procurement, many government jurisdictions do not allow negotiation of contracts that are above a certain value.

Instead, government jurisdictions generally require submittal of firm proposals that can be evaluated without negotiation and may be accepted or rejected. If selection is based on best value, most government jurisdictions limit the scope of negotiation to the seller's technical proposal, unless the category of work is professional services. After separate negotiations with each seller, which are limited to discussion of its technical proposal, sellers may be invited to submit a revised proposal representing the seller's best and final offer (see also Section 12.4.2.4 of the *PMBOK® Guide*—Third Edition).

.5 **Seller Rating Systems**

See Section 12.4.2.5 of the *PMBOK® Guide*—Third Edition.

.6 **Expert Judgment**

See Section 12.4.2.6 of the *PMBOK® Guide*—Third Edition.

.7 Proposal Evaluation Techniques

In government procurement, potential sellers submit sealed proposals that are opened publicly at a pre-established time and location. A seller's proposal is rejected if it is late or non-responsive. A proposal is non-responsive if it includes qualifications or conditions, is not submitted in the required format, or is not accompanied by the required documents (e.g., bid security). Governments also reserve the right to reject all proposals received, and proposals become the property of the government. Potential sellers whose proposals are not accepted are notified in writing after the selection of the successful seller.

When demonstrations or oral presentations (also known as interviews) are a part of the process, government may elect to make them either mandatory or optional. In such an interview, each potential seller presents the contents of its proposal and clarifies or explains any unusual or significant elements it includes. Potential sellers are not allowed to alter or amend their proposals after submission. Neither are potential sellers allowed to conduct negotiations during the interview process. A "best business practice" calls for each panelist to prepare his or her list of questions so that the same questions are asked of each potential seller (see also Section 12.4.2.7 of the *PMBOK® Guide*—Third Edition).

.8 Award and Preference Laws

Representative bodies often use preferences in procurement to achieve social and economic goals. Preferences may be a percentage target or "goal," or an absolute restriction. Some examples of preferences include:

- **Geographic preference.** In some government jurisdictions, a local seller has preference over a non-local seller. This preference may be applied by a national government giving preference to its own nationals or by a regional or local government, giving preference to regional or local firms. However, national governments that are signatories to the WTO Agreement on Government Procurement and the provincial governments within such nations may not discriminate against foreign or non-resident sellers by establishing preferences.
- **Population groups.** Many governments give a preference to a particular population group as a form of affirmative action. A preference may be in the form of a set aside or minimum target or goal for participation. These population groups may be minorities, other people who are deemed to be disadvantaged (e.g., women and disabled people), or people to whom the voters feel indebted (e.g., military veterans).
- **Small businesses.** Many governments give a preference to small businesses to foster growth in the economy.

.9 Protest and Grievance Procedures

Each governing body has administrative procedures for sellers to file grievances and protests related to an award. In summary, the seller identifies each issue in a written communication to the government agency. After reviewing those issues, the government agency sends a written response to the seller. If the response from the agency does not satisfy the firm, an informal meeting or formal hearing is scheduled. However, final decisions are the agency's responsibility. The seller must exhaust the administrative process before proceeding through the court system.

12.4.3 Select Sellers: Outputs

See Section 12.4.3 of the *PMBOK® Guide*—Third Edition.

12.5 Contract Administration

See Section 12.5 of the *PMBOK® Guide*—Third Edition.

12.5.1 Contract Administration: Inputs

Section 12.5.1 of the *PMBOK® Guide*—Third Edition discusses six inputs to the process of Contract Administration. One of these inputs requires information unique to government procurement, and a seventh input has been added with special application to government projects:

.1 Contract

See Section 12.5.1.1 of the *PMBOK® Guide*—Third Edition.

.2 Contract Management Plan

See Section 12.5.1.2 of the *PMBOK® Guide*—Third Edition.

.3 Selected Sellers

See Section 12.5.1.3 of the *PMBOK® Guide*—Third Edition.

.4 Performance Reports

See Section 12.5.1.4 of the *PMBOK® Guide*—Third Edition.

.5 Approved Change Requests

See Section 12.5.1.5 of the *PMBOK® Guide*—Third Edition.

.6 Work Performance Information

In government procurement, the seller submits invoices or requests for payment on a periodic basis (e.g., monthly) as specified in the contract. Most government agencies are subject to "prompt payment" laws or regulations that require payment of the undisputed amount of an invoice in a prompt manner (see also Section 12.5.1.6 of the *PMBOK® Guide*—Third Edition).

.7 Claims

If the government agency rejects a contract change requested by the contractor, this rejection can potentially lead to the filing of a claim by the seller. A rejected contract change request is also known as a potential claim. The project manager is responsible for attempting the early resolution of disputes before they become actual claims.

12.5.2 Contract Administration: Tools and Techniques

Section 12.5.2 of the *PMBOK® Guide*—Third Edition discusses tools and techniques for Contract Administration. Comments have been added to two of these, relative to government procurement. Also, one additional tool is shown, with particular public sector application.

.1 Contract Change Control System

See Section 12.5.2.1 of the *PMBOK® Guide*—Third Edition.

.2 Buyer-Conducted Performance Review

See Section 12.5.2.2 of the *PMBOK® Guide*—Third Edition.

.3 Inspections and Audits

Depending on the type of contract, there are various inspection clauses. The government retains the right to inspect project deliverables for compliance to requirements prior to acceptance. The responsible agency has a duty to the voters and taxpayers to ensure that it has received the contracted goods and services, and that these goods and services meet the specifications.

.4 Performance Reporting

See Section 12.5.2.4 of the *PMBOK® Guide*—Third Edition.

.5 Payment System

See Section 12.5.2.5 of the *PMBOK® Guide*—Third Edition.

.6 Claims Administration

In government procurement, a government agency generally has a structured dispute resolution process for unresolved claims. However, the process of dispute resolution can require up to several years before a final resolution (see also Section 12.5.2.6 of the *PMBOK® Guide*—Third Edition).

.7 Records Management System

See Section 12.5.2.7 of the *PMBOK® Guide*—Third Edition.

.8 Information Technology

See Section 12.5.2.8 of the *PMBOK® Guide*—Third Edition.

.9 Prevailing Wages

Some governments require that sellers on a public works project pay their employees the prevailing wage at the geographic location of the project. In many government jurisdictions, prevailing wage is defined as the "modal" average. When so defined, the prevailing wage represents the wage paid to the largest number of people in the job classification in the geographic area. However, the prevailing wage may also be defined as the average of the wages paid to all people in the job classification. The principle of the prevailing wage requirement is to level the playing field between sellers. Each seller can seek to lower costs through managing the project more efficiently, rather than simply cutting the wages of its employees.

12.5.3 Contract Administration: Outputs

See Section 12.5.3 of the *PMBOK® Guide*—Third Edition.

12.6 Contract Closure

See Section 12.6 of the *PMBOK® Guide*—Third Edition.

12.6.1 Contract Closure: Inputs

See Section 12.6.1 of the *PMBOK® Guide*—Third Edition.

12.6.2 Contract Closure: Tools and Techniques

Section 12.6.2 of the *PMBOK® Guide*—Third Edition discusses two tools and techniques for Contract Closure. Comments have been added to these, relative to government procurement. Also, a third tool has been added, with particular application to the public sector.

.1 Procurement Audits

As stated in the *PMBOK® Guide*—Third Edition, "A procurement audit is a structured review of the procurement process from the Plan Purchases and Acquisitions process (Section 12.1) through Contract Administration (Section 12.5). The objective of a procurement audit is to identify successes and failures that warrant recognition in the preparation or administration of other procurement contracts on the project, or on other projects within the performing organization."

In government procurement, a procurement audit would also address the following:
- Utilization compliance review (e.g., small business)
- Compliance with government policies review (e.g., competitive selection).

.2 Records Management System

See Section 12.6.2.2 of the *PMBOK® Guide*—Third Edition.

.3 De-Obligation of Funds

In government procurement, contract closure also allows the government agency to de-obligate any remaining funds (and redirect funds to other contracts for the approved project) and, where appropriate, return funds to the fund source. De-obligation of funds is also known as un-encumbering of funds.

12.6.3 Contract Closure: Outputs

Section 12.6.3 of the *PMBOK® Guide*—Third Edition discusses outputs for Contract Closure, all of which apply to government projects. Two new aspects that have particular application in government projects have been added:

.1 Closed Contracts

See Section 12.6.3.1 of the *PMBOK® Guide*—Third Edition.

.2 Organizational Process Assets (Updates)

See also Section 12.6.3.2 of the *PMBOK® Guide*—Third Edition.
- **Utilization compliance reports.** A final utilization report of population groups and small businesses (see Section 12.4.2.8) is prepared by sellers and submitted to the government agency for use in tabulating statistics for the government agency as a whole.
- **Policies compliance report.** Other reports may be prepared by a government agency regarding compliance with government policies and procedures for transmittal to the funding agency, and a narrative description of lessons learned, if any, for future use in similar projects.

Section IV

Appendices

Appendix A

Changes from Previous Edition of Government Extension

The purpose of this appendix is to provide a summary description of the most important changes to the *Government Extension to a Guide to the Project Management Body of Knowledge* (PMBOK® Guide—2000 Edition) in order to create the current edition.

Alignment with *PMBOK*® *Guide*—Third Edition

The current edition of the *Government Extension* was aligned in structure, style, and content with the. PMBOK® Guide—Third Edition. As the two documents should be used together for government projects, the alignment enables easier reference to the corresponding sections in each document. The process names and designations were updated to match the changes introduced in the PMBOK® Guide—Third Edition to enable consistency and clarity.

Chapter 1—Introduction Changes

Section 1.1 *Purpose of the Government Extension* was expanded to describe the need for and the goals of this standard. A new subsection was added to describe the target audience for the Government Extension.

Section 1.2 *What Makes Government Projects Unique?* became Section 1.2.4 under the new Section 1.2 *What is a Project?*. Section 1.2.4 was significantly revised to clearly describe the distinctive characteristics of public sector projects.

Section 1.3 *Project Management in the Government Context* describes management of projects in public sector environment, instead of referencing the corresponding section in PMBOK® Guide—Third Edition.

Section 1.6 *Project Management Context* was substantially changed. As programs have a much more expanded role in public than in private sector, this section includes a detailed explanation of the role and particularities of programs in the context of the governmental environment.

Section 1.7 *Government Extension Processes: Inputs, Tools, Techniques, and Outputs* was added as a new section and illustrates the alignment of processes with the PMBOK® Guide—Third Edition.

Chapter 2—Project Life Cycle and Organization Changes

The title and structure of Chapter 2 were aligned with *PMBOK® Guide*—Third Edition to better reflect its focus and content. A major content update was made to Section 2.3 *Organizational Influences,* representing a substantial revision from the *Government Extension*—2000 Edition. Section 2.3 now provides a detailed description of how organizational influences affect projects in the public sector.

Chapter 3—Project Management Processes for a Project Changes

As in the earlier edition of *Government Extension,* this chapter references the corresponding chapters in the*PMBOK® Guide*—Third Edition because project management in the government sector utilizes the same Project Management Process Groups as in the private sector.

Chapter 4—Project Integration Management Changes

The *Government Extension* was aligned with the *PMBOK® Guide*—Third Edition. Accordingly, four new integrative project management processes were added in the *PMBOK® Guide*—Third Edition,. Moreover, due to significant expansion of the content of this chapter in the *PMBOK® Guide,* most of the considerations included in *Government Extension*—2000 Edition are no longer applicable and have been deleted.

Section 4.1 *Develop Project Charter* describes common reasons to initiate a public sector project as inputs in the project charter elaboration process.

Section 4.7 *Close Project* introduces an additional organizational process asset, "project files," which has particular relevance in the government environment.

Chapter 5—Project Scope Management Changes

Section 5.1 *Initiation Government Extension*—2000 Edition was moved under Chapter 4 as Section 4.1 *Develop Project Charter.* Section 5.1 *Scope Planning* introduces the two overarching controls of scope planning for public sector projects: spending authority and public accountability.

Section 5.2 *Scope Definition* describes that some projects have unique scope definition challenges in the context of citizen-driven activity.

Section 5.3 *Create WBS,* of the current edition of the *Government Extension* adds an input "stakeholders analysis."

Section 5.4 *Scope Verification* introduces specific project controls such as compliance and public accountability, as well as a new output "communication artifacts".

Section 5.5 *Scope Control* describes an input "external influences," mostly sociopolitical, on scope control.

Chapter 6—Project Time Management Changes

Section 6.4 *Activity Duration Estimating* introduces an input "activity resource requirements" comprising preference laws, further detailed in Section 12.4.2.8.

Section 6.5 *Schedule Development* describes input "project scope statement" that reflects the annual budget cycle as a unique constraint for government projects and input "line item projects" that have specific constraints on project schedules. This section also describes a particular tool and technique, "obligations," intended to address the annual budget cycle constraint.

Chapter 7—Project Cost Management Changes

Chapter 7 was significantly reviewed in the current *Government Extension* to reflect significant tend changes in government arena.

Section 7.2 *Cost Budgeting* adds input "annual budget cycle" as well as tools and techniques "split funds," "matching funds," "obligations," "counterpart funding," and "grants" used for budgeting government projects. It also discusses in detail the performance-based and gateway budgeting used more and more in public sector worldwide to compensate the deficiencies of annual budgeting.

Section 7.3 *Cost Control* describes the particularities of performance reports as an input to cost control from the internal and external stakeholder's perspective.

Chapter 8—Project Quality Management Changes

Section 8.1 *Quality Planning* was substantially revised to update the quality planning inputs. Performance based budgeting, listed as a specific quality planning tool in *Government Extension*—2000 Edition, was moved to Section 7.2 and treated as a specific budgeting tool.

Section 8.2 *Perform Quality Assurance* introduces input "regulatory requirements and guidance." This section also includes particular aspects of a tool and technique "quality audits" with particular relevance for government projects, and new output "notification of non-compliance (deficiencies)" which is not usually seen in the private sector.

Chapter 9—Project Human Resource Management Changes

Chapter 9 was aligned with the *PMBOK® Guide*—Third Edition, thus increasing the number of processes and revising the process names.

Section 9.1 *Human Resource Planning* lists inputs specific to the public sector that can limit flexibility in human resource planning. Input "civil service system," listed as an organizational planning input in the earlier *Government Extension*—2000 edition, was changed to the enterprise environmental factors input in Section *9.1 Human Resource Planning* in *PMBOK® Guide*—Third Edition.. Section 9.1 also describes output "authority" and the limit on delegation of key decisions in government projects.

Section 9.2 *Acquire Project Team* expands the discussion in the earlier edition of *Government Extension*—2000 edition regarding particular public sector tools and techniques such as negotiation and hybrid staffing.

Chapter 10—Project Communications Management Changes

Section 10.1 *Communications Planning* was aligned with *PMBOK® Guide*—Third Edition with significant discussions regarding the particular inputs and tools and techniques used in government projects with consideration for external stakeholders and the general public.

Section 10.2 *Information Distribution* describes particular tools, techniques and outputs for public sector projects to satisfy informational needs of the public.

Section 10.3 *Performance Reporting* reflects the specific impacts of status reviews and recommended corrective actions over public sector projects through budget and funding adjustments.

Section 10.4 *Manage Stakeholders* is focused on information distribution in the government projects to legislative bodies and general public as specific stakeholders of public sector projects.

Chapter 11—Project Risk Management Changes

Section 11.1 *Risk Management Planning* continues to describe input "laws and regulations" as limitations on government projects by defining risks that the citizens will not accept. The section also adds a new output "political risk" while *Government Extension*—2000 edition considered political risk as an input to the risk identification process.

In Section 11.2 *Risk Identification* the description of information gathering tools and techniques are maintained and adjusted to reflect current terminology.

In Section 11.3 *Qualitative Risk Analysis* the discussion tool and technique "public review" was revised to better reflect current government practices around the world.

Section 11.4 *Quantitative Risk Analysis* describes an input "project environmental management plans" that address social and environmental concerns for public sector projects.

Chapter 12—Project Procurement Management Changes

The structure of Chapter 12 was aligned with the *PMBOK® Guide*—Third Edition including the revision of the process names.

Section 12.1 *Plan Purchases and Acquisitions* lists the same inputs as *PMBOK® Guide*—Third Edition with additional considerations for enterprise environmental factors and organizational process assets. This section, under tools and techniques, also includes an expanded discussion of additional categories of contract types used by government but not necessarily in private sector projects and degrees of competition and degrees of qualifications. This section also adds considerations to output "procurement management plan."

Section 12.2 *Plan Contracting* section adds "standard forms" to the list of tools and techniques used by government projects.

Section 12.3 *Request Seller Responses* includes expanded comments regarding government tools and techniques such as "bidder conferences" and "advertising," and adds "qualified sellers list as both a tool and technique and an output used frequently at various levels of government.

Section 12.4 *Select Sellers* is revised to align the tools and techniques with the corresponding section in *PMBOK® Guide*—Third Edition and describes through their particular application in the government environment including "proposal evaluation techniques," "award and preference laws," and "protest and grievance procedures."

Section 12.5 *Contract Administration* describes selected inputs, tools, and techniques, and outputs from the *PMBOK® Guide*—Third Edition and highlights their particular application in government projects as well as new input "claims" and new tool and technique "prevailing wages." Section 12.6 *Contract Closure* describes the applicability of the tools and techniques listed in the corresponding section of the *PMBOK® Guide*—Third Edition to government projects, and adds "de-obligation of funds" as a specific tool and technique used in public sector.

Appendix B

Evolution of PMI's *Government Extension to the PMBOK® Guide Third Edition*

B.1 Initial Development

In October 1998, the Project Management Institute (PMI) Government Specific Interest Group (SIG) appointed Nigel Blampied as project manager to develop a Government Extension. Over the course of the following year, articles were published in the SIG newsletter both to recruit team members and to begin a discussion on the features that make government projects unique.

A project work breakdown structure was prepared in September 1999; the PMI Standards Member Advisory Group approved a project charter in January 2000 establishing the Government Extension Project as a PMI Standards Project.

The team began to assemble in August 1999, mainly in response to articles in the SIG newsletter. All team members were volunteers, and they came from eight countries. The team included project managers from all spheres of government (national, regional, and local) and from several fields, including agriculture, education, energy, health and human services, labor, and transportation.

Each team member was asked to join one or more of the twelve chapter teams, and a lead author was assigned to each chapter. Lead authors were responsible for the successful completion of a particular chapter and wrote the first draft of the chapter. Co-authors contributed ideas and text to the chapter.

Draft 1 of each chapter was submitted to the full team as it was completed, between July and November 2000. The team evaluated 123 proposed amendments and approved 91 amendments.

In December 2000, Draft 2 was submitted to all members of the Government SIG with known email addresses. SIG members responded with 173 recommended amendments. A core team evaluated these proposed amendments, approved 153 and decided that 20 were unpersuasive. Draft 2 with the 153 amendments became Draft 3.

Draft 3 was reviewed by the PMI Standards Program Member Advisory Group and a panel of Subject Matter Experts (SME) in July 2001. The panel reviewed the draft and proposed thirteen specific amendments. Draft 3 with the eleven amendments became Draft 4, the exposure draft. The PMI Standards Program Member Advisory

Group sent the draft and the SME comments back to the team and requested the team consider how to handle each comment and recommendation.

Under the auspices of the PMI Standards Program, PMI published the exposure draft on the PMI Web site on 19 October 2001. Comments were received until 21 December 2001. A total of 95 recommended amendments were submitted. A core team evaluated these proposed amendments, approved 67, adopted 17 in a modified form and decided that 11 were unpersuasive. Draft 4 with the 84 amendments became the final draft. The project team submitted their final draft to the PMI Standards Manager in March 2002 for review and recommendation by the PMI Standards Program Member Advisory Group to publish as a PMI Standard.

B.2   2004–2005 Update

On April 29, 2004 the PMI Standards Program chartered a project to produce a second edition of the *Government Extension*. Peter Dimov, PMP, was appointed as project manager. Whereas the first edition aligned with the *A Guide to the Project Management Body of Knowledge—2000 Edition (PMBOK® Guide—2000 Edition)*, the second edition was to align with *A Guide to the Project Management Body of Knowledge—Third Edition (PMBOK® Guide—Third Edition)*.

A 35-member team began to assemble in spring–summer 2004. Team members are listed in Appendix C. All team members are volunteers, and they come from all spheres of government—national, regional, and local—and from a large number of industries.

Team members joined one or more of ten teams: Core Team; Communications; Membership; Process Definition and Lessons Learned; *PMBOK® Guide*—Third Edition Alignment and Additions; Editorial and Writing, Glossary; Comments; Government Review; and Product Review. The *PMBOK® Guide*—Third Edition Alignment and Additions, the principal development team, was further sub-divided into twelve sub teams, one for each chapter.

The Core Team met in Washington DC for two days in late August 2004, reviewed the differences between the 2000 Edition and the Third Edition of the *PMBOK® Guide*. The project manager and a core team member from the team participated in this review. The Core Team considered how the *PMBOK® Guide* changes might affect the *Government Extension*. This led to an initial list of probable changes.

Building on the work of the Core Team, each chapter sub-team brainstormed recommended changes. In September 2004 they produced the first list of changes, which was reviewed by the PMBOK Alignment and Additions team. In November and December 2004 each chapter sub-team further detailed the approved changes. The first draft, incorporating the agreed changes, was produced in January 2005.

The entire GEU team reviewed the first draft to ensure consistency between chapters. The Core Team met in February 2005 to analyze the first draft and the team's observations. The first draft with the updates produced by the Core Team became a second draft, which was submitted to the PMI Standards Program Manager.

After a review by the PMI Standards Program Member Advisory Group, the second draft was submitted to a panel of Subject Matter Experts (SME). The panel reviewed the draft, gave it a positive review, and recommended that it proceed to the exposure draft. Panel members proposed 43 amendments, and the team incorporated 27 of these into the document. Draft 2 with the amendments became the exposure draft.

Under the auspices of the PMI Standards Program, PMI published the exposure draft on the PMI Web site in July 2005. Comments were received until 12 September 2005. A total of 133 recommended amendments were submitted. The chapter teams evaluated these proposed amendments, accepted 105, accepted 23 with modifications, deferred 1, and decided that 4 were not accepted. The exposure draft with the 128 amendments became the final draft.

The project team submitted their final draft to the PMI Standards Manager in February 2006 for review and recommendation by the PMI Standards Program Member Advisory Group to publish as a PMI Standard.

Appendix C

Contributors and Reviewers of *Government Extension to the PMBOK® Guide Third Edition*

PMI volunteers first attempted to codify the Project Management Body of Knowledge in the Special Report on Ethics, Standards, and Accreditation, published in 1983. Since that time, other volunteers have come forward to update and improve that original document and contribute the now de facto standard for project management, PMI's, *A Guide to the Project Management Body of Knowledge (PMBOK® Guide)*.

The *PMBOK® Guide* addresses knowledge and practices "generally recognized as good practice on most of the projects most of the time". Extensions of *A Guide to the Project Management Body of Knowledge (PMBOK® Guide)* strive to describe project management knowledge and practice in a particular industry or type of project.

The *Government Extension to the PMBOK® Guide—2000 Edition* describes knowledge and practices that are "generally recognized as good practice" for government projects most of the time. It is applicable to worldwide government projects at the national, state/provincial, and local levels.

This Appendix describes specific contributions of many of the individuals listed below and should be consulted for further information about individual contributions to the project. The Project Management Institute is grateful to all of these individuals for their support and acknowledges their contributions to the project management profession.

C.1 Project Team Organization

Initially a Leadership Team was formed to perform detailed project analysis, planning and a high level outline of the *Government Extension to the PMBOK® Guide—Third Edition*. Upon completion of these deliverables, the team dissolved and was succeeded by a Project Core Team. The rest of the project team was divided by Chapter Teams as well as Functional Teams.

The following individuals served as team members and contributors.

Project Manager
Peter Dimov PMP, CBM

Leadership Team
Peter Dimov, PMP, CBM - PM
Mike Musial, PMP, CBM - Deputy PM
Petya Alexandrova, PMP
Larry Oliva, PMP
Nigel Blampied, PMP
Will Brimberry

Core Team
Peter Dimov, PMP, CBM - PM
Mike Musial, PMP, CBM - Deputy PM
Petya Alexandrova, PMP
Larry Oliva, PMP
Nigel Blampied, PMP
Kenyon Potter, PE

Chapter Teams

Chapter 1 Introduction
LEAD: Bobbi Markley
George Jucan
James Wattnem

Chapter 2 Project Life Cycle and Organization
LEAD: Betty O'Connor
Kenyon Potter, PE
Bobbi Markley

Chapter 3 Project Management Processes
LEAD: Ned C. Storey
Greg F. Miller
James Wattnem

Chapter 4 Project Integration Management
LEAD: Ned C. Storey
Greg F. Miller

Chapter 5 Project Scope Management
LEAD: George Jucan
Bobbi Markley
Kenyon Potter, PE

Chapter 6 Project Time Management
LEAD: Khalid Khan
Betty O'Connor
Ivan Kenna

Chapter 7 Project Cost Management
LEAD: Barbara J. Marshall
Greg F. Miller
Betty O'Connor

Chapter 8 Project Quality Management
LEAD: Greg Bluher
Ruth H. Vandegrift
Bill Motley

Chapter 9 Project Human Resource Management
LEAD: Ivan Kenna
Barbara J. Marshall

Chapter 10 Project Communications Management
LEAD: George Jucan
Khalid Khan
Benjamin Terry Williams

Chapter 11 Project Risk Management
LEAD: Greg F. Miller
Bobbi Markley
Kenyon Potter, PE
Ruth H. Vandegrift

Chapter 12 Project Procurement Management
LEAD: Kenyon Potter, PE
George Jucan
Betty O'Connor
Benjamin Terry Williams

Functional Teams

Editorial Team
Ned C. Storey, (Chair)
George Jucan
Bobbi Markley
Benjamin Terry Williams

Glossary Team
Kenyon Potter, PE (Chair)
Foster, Luke J.

Comments Team
Daniel K. Frisby
Ruth H. Vandegrift

Government Review
Nigel Blampied, (Chair)
Gregory Bluher
Daniel K. Frisby
Kenyon Potter, PE
Daniel A. Rivers

Product Review
Gregory Bluher
Daniel K. Frisby
Ruth H. Vandegrift

C.2 Project Team Members

The complete list of the project team members in alphabetical order is provided below:

Petya Alexandrova
David Baker
Nigel Blampied
Peter Ivanov Dimov
DJ Everette
Douglas Findley
Kevin Flanagan
Luke Foster
Daniel Frisby
Annette Hobbs
George Jucan
Ivan Rikard Kenna
Khalid Ahmad Khan
Bobbi Markley
Barbara Marshall

Jorge Alberto Mathias de Almeida
Gregory Miller
Mark Moore
Barry Morrison
Mike Musial
Betty O'Connor
Lawrence Oliva
Kenyon Potter
Dinakar Prabhakar
Daniel Alvin Rivers
Ned Storey
Jeffrey Trombly
Ruth Vandegrift
James Wattnem

C.3 Significant Contributors

In addition to the members of the Project Leadership Team, the Project Core Team, the Chapter Team and the Functional Teams, the following individuals provided significant input or concepts:

Will Brimberry
Margareth Carneiro
George Jucan
Ivan Kenna

Bobbi Markley
Barbara Marshall
Larry Sieck

C.4 Exposure Draft Reviewers and Contributors

In addition to team members, the following individuals provided recommendations for improving the Exposure Draft of the Government Extension to A PMBOK® Guide— Third Edition:

Hussain Ali Al-Anasari
Mahd Ablulla Al-Kuwari
Mohammed Safi Batley
Nigel Blampied
Bernardo Bustamante

Brenda Breslin
John E. Cormier
Rebecca Winston
William Zimmer

C.5 PMI Standards Program Member Advisory Group

The following individuals served as members of the PMI Standards Program Member Advisory Group during development of the *Government Extension to the PMBOK® Guide—Third Edition:*

Julia M. Bednar, PMP
Thomas Kurihara
Bobbye Underwood, PMP
Carol Holliday, PMP
Debbie O'Bray

Asbjorn Rolstadas, PhD
David Ross, PMP
Cindy Stackpole, PMP
Dave Violette, MPM, PMP

C.6 Production Staff

Special mention is due to the following employees of PMI:

Ruth Anne Guerrero, PMP, Standards Manager
Dottie Nichols, PMP, Former Standards Manager
Steven L. Fahrenkrog, PMP, Director, Knowledge Delivery
Dan Goldfischer, Editor-in-Chief
Donn Greenberg, Manager, Publications
Richard E. Schwartz, Product Editor
Kristin L. Vitello, Standards Project Specialist
Barbara Walsh, Publications Planner
Nan Wolfslayer, Standards Project Specialist

C.7 Special Thanks

The Project Team expresses our gratitude to Robbins-Gioia, LLC and its Senior Vice President, Emory Miller, for supporting the brainstorming phase of our work and providing needed space and resources.

Appendix D

Application Area Extensions

D.1 Need for Application Area Extensions

Application area extensions are necessary when there are generally accepted knowledge and practices for a category of projects in one application area that are not generally accepted across the full range of project types in most application areas. Application area extensions reflect:

- Unique or unusual aspects of the project environment of which the project management team must be aware, in order to manage the project efficiently and effectively.
- Common knowledge and practices that, if followed, will improve the efficiency and effectiveness of the project (e.g., standard work breakdown structures).

Application area-specific knowledge and practices can arise as a result of many factors, including, but not limited to, differences in cultural norms, technical terminology, societal impact, or project life cycles. For example:

- In construction, where virtually all work is accomplished under contract, there are common knowledge and practices related to procurement that do not apply to all categories of projects.
- In bioscience, there are common knowledge and practices driven by the regulatory environment that do not apply to all categories of projects
- In government contracting, there are common knowledge and practices driven by government acquisition regulations that do not apply to all categories of projects
- In consulting, there are common knowledge and practices created by the project manager's sales and marketing responsibilities that do not apply to all categories of projects.

Application area extensions are:

- Additions to the core material of *PMBOK® Guide*—Third Edition, Chapters 1 through 12—not substitutes for it.
- Organized in a fashion similar to the *PMBOK® Guide*—Third Edition, that is, by identifying and describing the project management processes unique to that application area.
- Unique additions to the core material. Such content may:
  - Identify new or modified processes
  - Subdivide existing processes
  - Describe different sequences or interactions of processes
  - Increase elements or modifying the common process definitions
  - Define special inputs, tools and techniques, and/or outputs for the existing processes.

Application area extensions are *not*:
- "How-to" documents or "practice guidelines"—such documents may be issued as PMI Standards, but they are not what are intended as extensions.
- A lower level of detail than is addressed in the *PMBOK® Guide*—Third Edition. Such details may be addressed in handbooks or guidebooks that may be issued as PMI Standards, but they are not what is intended as extensions.

D.2 Criteria for Development of Application Area Extensions

Extensions will be developed under the following criteria:
- There is a substantial body of knowledge that is both project-oriented and unique or nearly unique to that application area.
- There is an identifiable PMI component (e.g., a PMI Specific Interest Group, College, or Chapter) or an identifiable external organization willing and able to commit the necessary resources to subscribe to and support the PMI Standards Program with the development and maintenance of a specific PMI Standard or the extension may be developed by PMI itself.
- The proposed extension is able to pass the same level of rigorous PMI Project Management Standard-Setting Process as any other PMI Standard.

D.3 Publishing and Format of Application Area Extensions

Application area extensions are developed and/or published by PMI, or they are developed and/or published by either a PMI component or an external organization under a formal agreement with PMI.
- Extensions match the *PMBOK® Guide* in style and content. They use the same paragraph and subparagraph numbers for the material that has been extended.
- Sections and paragraphs of the *PMBOK® Guide* that are not extended are not repeated in extensions.
- Extensions contain a rationale/justification about the need for an extension and its material.
- Extensions are delimited in terms of what they are not intended to do.

D.4 Process for Development and Maintenance of Application Area Extensions

When approved in accordance with the PMI Standards-Setting Process, application area extensions become PMI standards. They will be developed and maintained in accordance with the process described below.
- An extension must be sponsored by PMI, a formally chartered PMI component (e.g., a Specific Interest Group, College, or Chapter), or another organization external to PMI, which has been approved by the PMI Standards Program Member Advisory Group and the PMI Standards Manager. Co-sponsorship with PMI is the preferred arrangement. All approvals will be by formal written agreement between PMI and the sponsoring entity; such agreement will include, among other things, the parties' agreement as to intellectual property ownership rights and publications rights to the extension.

- A project to develop, publish, and/or maintain an extension must be approved by the PMI Standards Program. Permission to initiate, develop, and maintain an extension must be received from PMI and will be the subject of an agreement between or among the organizations. If there is no other sponsoring organization, the PMI Standards Program may elect to proceed alone.
- The sponsoring group will notify and solicit advice and support from the PMI Standards Program Member Advisory Group and PMI Standards Manager throughout the development and maintenance process. They will concur with the appropriateness of the sponsoring organization for the proposed extension and will review the extension during its development to identify any conflicts or overlaps with other similar projects that may be under way.
- The sponsoring group will prepare a proposal to develop the extension. The proposal will include a justification for the project with a matrix of application-area specific processes and the affected sections of this document (i.e., the *PMBOK® Guide—Third Edition*). It will also contain the commitment of sufficient qualified drafters and reviewers; identification of funding requirements, including reproduction, postage, telephone costs, desktop publishing, etc.; commitment to the PMI procedures for PMI Standards extension development and maintenance; and a plan and schedule for extension development and maintenance.
- Following acceptance of the proposal, the project team will prepare a project charter for approval by the sponsoring group and the PMI Standards Program Team. The charter will include sources of funding and any funding proposed to be provided by PMI. It will include a requirement for periodic review of the extension with reports to the PMI Standards Program Team and a "Sunset Clause" that specifies when, and under what conditions, the extension will be removed from active status as a PMI Standard.
- The proposal will be submitted to the PMI Standards Manager in accordance with the PMI Standards-Setting Process. The PMI Standards Manager will determine if the proposal can be expected to result in a document that will meet the requirements for a PMI Standard and if adequate resources and sources of support have been identified. To help with this determination, the PMI Standards Manager will seek review and comment by the PMI Standards Program Member Advisory Group and, if appropriate, a panel of knowledgeable persons not involved with the extension.
- The PMI Standards Manager, with the support of the PMI Standards Program Member Advisory Group, will monitor and support the development of the approved project.
- The sponsoring organization will develop the extension according to the approved project charter, including coordinating with the PMI Standards Program Team for support, review, and comment.
- When the extension has been completed to the satisfaction of the sponsoring organization, it will be submitted to the PMI Standards Manager, who will manage the final approval and publication processes in accordance with the PMI Standards-Setting Process. This final submittal will include listing of, and commitment by, the sponsoring organization to the PMI extension maintenance processes and efforts.
- Following approval of the extension as a PMI Standard, the sponsoring organization will implement the extension maintenance process in accordance with the approved plan.

Appendix E

Additional Sources of Information

Project Management is a growing, dynamic field. This is also true of project management within government organizations.

E.1 Professional and Technical Organizations

This Government Extension to the *PMBOK Guide®*—Third Edition was developed and published by the Project Management Institute (PMI). PMI can be contacted at:

Project Management Institute
Four Campus Boulevard
Newtown Square, PA 19073-3299 USA
Phone: +1-610-356-4600
Fax: +1-610-356-4647
E-mail: pmihq@pmi.org
Internet: http://www.pmi.org

Refer to Appendix E.1 in the *PMBOK Guide®*—Third Edition for a list of professional and trade organizations that may be able to provide additional information about project management. In addition, there are other organizations that focus on issues relating to government organizations, which may be able to provide additional information about project management in government organizations. For your convenience, the relevant chapters are indicated to the right of the address.

Organization	Chapter No(s)
International Civil Service Commission (UNICSC) www.icsc.un.org	9
International Construction Information Society www.icis.org	5
International Cost Engineering Council www.icoste.org	7
International Institute of Administrative Sciences www.iiasiisa.be/iias/aiacc.htm	All
International Organization for Standardization (ISO) www.iso.org	8
International Risk Management Institute (IRMI) www.irmi.com	11
Project Management Institute, Government SIG www.pmi-govsig.org	All

(continued)

Organization	Chapter No(s)
World Trade Organization (WTO), Agreement on Government Procurement www.wto.org/english/tratop_e/gproc_e/gp_gpa_e.htm	12
United Nations Public Administration (UNPAN) www.unpan.org	All
United Nations Commission on Sustainable Development (UNCSD) www.un.org/esa/sustdev	All
World Bank www.worldbank.org	All

E.2 Commercial Publishers

Refer to Appendix E.2 in the *PMBOK Guide®*—Third Edition for a list of commercial publishers, in addition to PMI, that may be able to provide additional information about project management.

In addition, several publishers produce books and publications on project management in government organizations. Commercial publishers that produce such materials include:

American Bar Association (ABA)
American Society of Civil Engineers (ASCE)
International Institute of Administrative Sciences (IIAS)
National Institute of Governmental Purchasing, Inc (NIGP)

E.3 Product and Service Vendors

Refer to Appendix E.3 in the *PMBOK Guide®*—Third Edition.

E.4 Educational Institutions

Refer to Appendix E.4 in the *PMBOK Guide®*—Third Edition.

Appendix F

Summary of Project Management Knowledge Areas

Project Integration Management

Project Integration Management includes the processes and activities needed to identify, define, combine, unify, and coordinate the various processes and project management activities within the Project Management Process Groups. In the project management context, integration includes characteristics of unification, consolidation, articulation, and integrative actions that are crucial to project completion, successfully meeting customer and stakeholder requirements, and managing expectations. The Project Integration Management processes include:

- Develop Project Charter—developing the project charter that formally authorizes a project
- Develop Preliminary Project Scope Statement—developing the preliminary project scope statement that provides a high-level scope narrative
- Develop Project Management Plan—documenting the actions necessary to define, prepare, integrate, and coordinate all subsidiary plans into a project management plan
- Direct and Manage Project Execution—executing the work defined in the project management plan to achieve the project's requirements defined in the project scope statement
- Monitor and Control Project Work—monitoring and controlling the processes required to initiate, plan, execute, and close a project to meet the performance objectives defined in the project management plan
- Integrated Change Control—reviewing all change requests, approving changes, and controlling changes to the deliverables and organizational process assets
- Close Project—finalizing all activities across all of the Project Process Groups to formally close the project.

Project Scope Management

Project Scope Management includes the processes required to ensure that the project includes all the work required, and only the work required, to complete the project successfully. Project Scope Management is primarily concerned with defining and controlling what is and is not included in the project. The Project Scope Management processes include:

- Scope Planning—creating a project scope management plan that documents how the project scope will be defined, verified, and controlled, and how the work breakdown structure (WBS) will be created and defined
- Scope Definition—developing a detailed project scope statement as the basis for future project decisions
- Create WBS—subdividing the major project deliverables and project work into smaller, more manageable components
- Scope Verification—formalizing acceptance of the completed project deliverables
- Scope Control—controlling changes to the project scope.

Project Time Management

Project Time Management includes the processes required to accomplish timely completion of the project. The Project Time Management processes include:

- Activity Definition—identifying the specific schedule activities that need to be performed to produce the various project deliverables
- Activity Sequencing—identifying and documenting dependencies among schedule activities
- Activity Resource Estimating—estimating the type and quantities of resources required to perform each schedule activity
- Activity Duration Estimating—estimating the number of work periods that will be needed to complete individual schedule activities
- Schedule Development—analyzing activity sequences, durations, resource requirements, and schedule constraints to create the project schedule
- Schedule Control—controlling changes to the project schedule.

Project Cost Management

Project Cost Management includes the processes involved in planning, estimating, budgeting, and controlling costs so that the project can be completed within the approved budget. The Project Cost Management processes include:

- Cost Estimating—developing an approximation of the costs of the resources needed to complete project activities
- Cost Budgeting—aggregating the estimated costs of individual activities or work packages to establish a cost baseline
- Cost Control—influencing the factors that create cost variances and controlling changes to the project budget.

Project Quality Management

Project Quality Management includes the processes and activities of the performing organization that determine quality policies, objectives, and responsibilities so that the project will satisfy the needs for which it was undertaken. It implements the quality management system through policy and procedures, with continuous process improvement activities conducted throughout, as appropriate. The Project Quality Management processes include:

- Quality Planning—identifying which quality standards are relevant to the project and determining how to satisfy them
- Perform Quality Assurance—applying the planned, systematic quality activities to ensure that the project employs all processes needed to meet requirements
- Perform Quality Control—monitoring specific project results to determine whether they comply with relevant quality standards and identifying ways to eliminate causes of unsatisfactory performance.

Project Human Resource Management

Project Human Resource Management includes the processes that organize and manage the project team. The project team is comprised of the people who have assigned roles and responsibilities for completing the project. While it is common to speak of roles and responsibilities being assigned, team members should be involved in much of the project's planning and decision-making. Early involvement of team members adds expertise during the planning process and strengthens commitment to the project. The type and number of project team members can often change as the project progresses. Project team members can be referred to as the project's staff. Project Human Resource Management processes include:

- Human Resource Planning—Identifying and documenting project roles, responsibilities, and reporting relationships, as well as creating the staffing management plan
- Acquire Project Team—Obtaining the human resources needed to complete the project
- Develop Project Team—Improving the competencies and interaction of team members to enhance project performance
- Manage Project Team—Tracking team member performance, providing feedback, resolving issues, and coordinating changes to enhance project performance.

Project Communications Management

Project Communications Management includes the processes required to ensure timely and appropriate generation, collection, distribution, storage, retrieval, and ultimate disposition of project information. The Project Communications Management processes provide the critical links among people and information that are necessary for successful communications. Project managers can spend an inordinate amount of time communicating with the project team, stakeholders, customer, and sponsor. Everyone involved in the project should understand how communications affect the project as a whole. Project Communications Management processes include:

- Communications Planning—determining the information and communications needs of the project stakeholders

- Information Distribution—making needed information available to project stakeholders in a timely manner
- Performance Reporting—collecting and distributing performance information, including status reporting, progress measurement, and forecasting
- Manage Stakeholders—managing communications to satisfy the requirements of, and resolve issues with, project stakeholders.

Project Risk Management

Project Risk Management includes the processes concerned with conducting risk management planning, identification, analysis, responses, and monitoring and control on a project. The objectives of Project Risk Management are to increase the probability and impact of positive events and decrease the probability and impact of events adverse to project objectives. Project Risk Management processes include:

- Risk Management Planning—deciding how to approach, plan, and execute the risk management activities for a project
- Risk Identification—determining which risks might affect the project and documenting their characteristics
- Qualitative Risk Analysis—prioritizing risks for subsequent further analysis or action by assessing and combining their probability of occurrence and impact
- Quantitative Risk Analysis—numerically analyzing the effect on overall project objectives of identified risks
- Risk Response Planning—developing options and actions to enhance opportunities and to reduce threats to project objectives
- Risk Monitoring and Control—tracking identified risks, monitoring residual risks, identifying new risks, executing risk response plans, and evaluating their effectiveness throughout the project life cycle.

Project Procurement Management

Project Procurement Management includes the processes to purchase or acquire the products, services, or results needed from outside the project team to perform the work. This chapter presents two perspectives of procurement. The organization can be either the buyer or seller of the product, service, or results under a contract.

Project Procurement Management includes the contract management and change control processes required to administer contracts or purchase orders issued by authorized project team members. Project Procurement Management also includes administering any contract issued by an outside organization (the buyer) that is acquiring the project from the performing organization (the seller) and administering contractual obligations placed on the project team by the contract. Project Procurement Management processes include:

- Plan Purchases and Acquisitions—determining what to purchase or acquire, and determining when and how
- Plan Contracting—documenting products, services, and results requirements and identifying potential sellers
- Request Seller Responses—obtaining information, quotations, bids, offers, or proposals, as appropriate
- Select Sellers—reviewing offers, choosing from among potential sellers, and negotiating a written contract with a seller

- Contract Administration—managing the contract and the relationship between the buyer and the seller, reviewing and documenting how a seller is performing or has performed to establish required corrective actions and provide a basis for future relationships with the seller, managing contract related changes and, when appropriate, managing the contractual relationship with the outside buyer of the project
- Contract Closure—completing and settling each contract, including the resolution of any open items, and closing each contract.

Section V

Glossary and Index

Glossary

Index by Keyword

Glossary

Advertisement. A formal notice of a government contracting opportunity intended to ensure full and open competition. The notice is typically published in a newspaper of general circulation and/ or publications of professional societies, as well as contract registers of government bodies.

Appropriation. An action by a government body to provide funding for a line item project or a program. Appropriations are typically contained in the budget of the governmental body, but may also be enacted separately. See also *Line Item Projects* and *Program*.

Best Value Selection. A selection process in which proposals submitted by potential sellers are evaluated using several factors including the seller's price. Each seller receives a quantitative point score for each factor except for price, which is already quantified. The process often involves assigning a predetermined weight to each factor; however, a government body may elect not to assign a weight to price. If a weight is assigned to price, a contract is awarded to the seller with the best weighted score. If a weight is not assigned to price, each seller's price can be divided by the weighted score of other factors and the contract awarded to the seller with the lowest price per point. Alternatively, the selection process may perform an evaluation of sellers and determine which proposal is most advantageous to the government body without use of weights to combine factors.

Civil Service System. A system in which government employees hold office from one administration to another. Their positions are protected, provided that they remain politically neutral. See also *Spoils System*.

Defined Contribution. Split funding by program where some fund source(s) contribute a fixed amount, with one source funding the balance. See also *Fund Source*.

Defined Elements of Work. Split funding by program where each fund source bears the cost of its portion(s) of the project on a percentage basis. See also *Fund Source*.

Devolution. Delegation of work or power by a national government to a regional or local government, or by a regional government to a local government.

Devolve. See *Devolution*.

Eminent Domain. A process that allows the government to take possession of private property when this is deemed to be in the best interests of the public.

Encumbrance. See *Obligation*.

Environmental Review. A process in which potential impacts to natural, cultural, historical, and community resources are identified and examined, and strategies are developed to mitigate any significant impacts. Environmental review typically culminates in the production of one or more environmental documents (e.g., EIR).

Full and Open Competition. A process in which all responsible sources are allowed to compete for a contract.

Fund Source. A source of funding for a government project. A project may have more than one fund source. Fund sources may include national, regional, and local governments, as well as other sources (e.g., banks and financial institutions).

Government Body. An assembly of people at the national, regional or local level, which deliberates and establishes applicable laws or regulations and administers government projects. In some jurisdictions, laws or regulations may also be known as "statutes" and "ordinances."

Government Transfer Payment. See *Obligation*.

Hybrid Staff. A mixture of civil service and contracted staff.

Indefinite Delivery Indefinite Quantity (IDIQ) Contracts. Contracts that state the type of service to be delivered, the length of time in which the service can be requested (generally five years or less), and the minimum and maximum contract amount, but give no project-specific information. Additionally, the contract typically includes a "price book" and each potential seller submits a markup or markdown in the form of a coefficient (e.g., 1.1 or 0.9).

Job Order Contract (JOC). See IDIQ contracts.

Line-Item Projects. Projects that are added to the budget of the government body on a project-by-project basis rather than as a program. See also *Appropriation*; compare to *Program*.

Local Government. A government body of a small geographic region within a nation. Local governments may or may not overlap geographically. When local governments overlap, they typically have differing duties. Examples of local governments include counties, cities, towns, municipalities, school boards, water boards, road boards, sanitation districts, electrification districts, fire protection districts, and hospital districts.

Lowest Responsible Seller. A responsible seller who submits the lowest bid or proposal that is responsive to the IFB or RFP, respectively. The selection process includes evaluation of each seller's proposal to ensure that it meets minimum qualifications of the government body. The degree of qualification may vary, but a seller must meet the minimum qualifications of the government body to be determined to be "responsible." For example, in construction contracts, the minimum qualifications are generally a contractor's license and a performance bond. For professional service contracts, a different selection process is used. See also *Responsible Seller*; compare to *Qualifications-Based Selection*.

Matching Funds. A form of split funding by program. When governments "devolve" project selection to lower government bodies, they often require those lower government bodies to pay a portion of the project cost. Matching funds may be apportioned on a percentage basis or as a defined contribution. See *Split Funding, Defined Contribution*, and *Defined Elements of Work*.

Multiple Award Schedules. A type of contract that can be used when there is a generally accepted "reasonable price" for a good or service. Multiple award schedules are particularly valuable for procurement of commodities. Each potential seller submits its qualifications and schedule of rates to the government body. Assuming each schedule of rates is based on generally accepted "reasonable" prices, the government body can select the seller that is most advantageous to the government. If these are approved, government agencies may buy goods and services at the published rates without a separate competition.

National Government. The government body of an internationally recognized nation. Examples of national governments include a confederation, federation, or unitary state.

Obligation. A budget process that places funds for a contract into a separate account that can be used only for the specific contract. The funds remain available for two to five years, depending on the rules set by the government body. This avoids the need to return to the government body and seek additional appropriation in each fiscal year. See also *Appropriation* and *Zero-Balance Budgeting*.

On-Call Contracts. See *Indefinite Delivery Indefinite Quantity Contracts*.

Opposition Stakeholders. Stakeholders who perceive themselves as being harmed if the project is successful.

Other Than Full and Open Competition. A process where one or more responsible sources is excluded from competing for a contract. Examples of this scenario include a set-aside for small disadvantaged businesses or small and a sole source contract. See also *Sole Source Contract*.

Percentage Split. Split funding by program where each program funds a percentage of the project.

Prevailing Wage. The prevailing wage is often the wage paid to the largest number of people in the job classification in the geographic area. When so defined, the prevailing wage represents the "modal" average. However, the prevailing wage may also be defined as the "mean" average of the wages paid to all people in the job classification.

Program. A group of projects managed in a coordinated way to obtain benefits not available by managing them individually. See also *Line Item Projects*.

Protest. A formal objection to the selection or award of a government contract to a seller by a disappointed seller or any other person. The formal objection typically must be filed during the selection process and comply with a mandatory procedure established by the government body.

Qualifications-Based Selection. A selection process in which the contract is awarded to the best-qualified seller among those who offer a reasonable price to the government. This approach is most often used on design contracts, where the design cost is a small fraction of the construction cost, but increased attention to design can result in large construction savings. Sellers' qualifications are evaluated, the sellers are ranked, and a contract is negotiated with the most qualified seller. If the government and the seller cannot agree on a reasonable price, the government terminates negotiations with the highest-ranked seller and begins negotiating with the next highest-ranked seller.

Regional Government. A government body of a large region within a nation. In small nations, there are often no regional governments—only a national government and local governments. In confederations and federations, the regional government has considerable autonomy. In unitary states, the regional government is subject to control by the national government. Examples of regional governments include states, provinces, departments, cantons, kingdoms, principalities, republics, regions, and territories.

Regulators. Individuals or organizations that must approve various aspects of the project. Regulators enforce rules and regulations. They are actively involved in the project, but generally have no interest in its success—it will not affect them. Regulators are either agents of a higher government or of another agency in the same government as the performing organization.

Responsible Seller. A seller that meets the minimum qualifications required by the government body to perform the work.

Sole Source Contract. A contract in which there is only a single seller that can accomplish the work—by reason of experience, possession of specialized facilities, or technical competence—in a time frame required by the government. See also *Other Than Full and Open Competition*.

Split Funding. A project that receives funding from multiple fund sources or from budgets in more than one budget year. See also *Matching Funds*, *Defined Contribution*, and *Defined Elements of Work*.

Spoils System. A system in which each new administration can replace government employees. See also *Civil Service System*.

Tight Matrix. A system in which each project has an assigned work area, and employees sit together in that area while they are working on the project, even though they do not report to the same supervisor.

Use It or Lose It. A provision in the annual budget of a government body that requires funds to be spent or obligated by the end of the fiscal year.

Weighted Price and Qualifications. See *Best Value Selection*.

Zero-Balance Budgeting. A budget process where each year's budget starts with a zero balance, requiring justification of every expense and income item. See also *Obligation*.

Index by Keyword